THE KEYS TO A
SUCCESSFUL
PRESIDENCY

Edited by Alvin S. Felzenberg

Published by The Heritage Foundation
214 Massachusetts Ave., NE
Washington, DC 20002
202-546-4400
www.heritage.org

Cover design by Bremmer & Goris Communications, Inc.,
Alexandria, Virginia

Interior photos by Chas Geer

ISBN: 0-89195-093-1

Printed in the United States of America

TABLE OF CONTENTS

ACKNOWLEDGMENTS

This book, and the public Mandate for Leadership 2000 programs on which it is based, was a collaborative effort of many people. While it is impossible to mention them all, some deserve particular recognition.

We owe a special thanks to former Attorney General Edwin Meese, currently Ronald Reagan Distinguished Fellow at The Heritage Foundation. Ed's generosity with his time, advice, and willingness always to go the extra mile assured the success of this project. He moderated six of the nine public programs and was a presenter at two. He brought to each task his deep knowledge of the presidency and the good cheer and wisdom that was evident in every post he held over the course of several decades of public service.

My thanks also go to Executive Vice President Phil Truluck and Vice Presidents Stuart Butler and Kim Holmes of The Heritage Foundation. Each was indispensable to the endeavor, providing guidance and offering sound suggestions. Their assistance was invaluable in helping me to cull the ideas and draw out the most illustrative quotes from the hundreds of pages of transcripts from the Heritage forums that form the heart of this book. Heritage Foundation President Edwin Feulner and Vice President Mike Franc provided invaluable additional advice on the selection of speakers for the events.

Many individuals at Heritage helped to make the public events successful, including Julene Haworth, David Cole, Ryan Ellis, Matt Spalding, Melissa Naudin, Emily Stimpson, Cathi Smith, Melinda Brown, Allison Klucas, and Viktoria Ziebarth.

Vice President Herb Berkowitz and Kristine Bershers helped spread the word about the Mandate project to the public; Andrew Blasko helped assemble photographs; John Dickson posted the nine transcripts on the Web.

Special thanks for assuring the quality of this publication go to Angela Antonelli, David Cole, Dan Fisk, Bill Poole, Jan Smith, Leslie Greenberg, Richard Odermatt, Thomas Timmons, Michelle Smith, and Anne Gartland.

Last, but hardly least, I want to express my deep appreciation to each of the presenters and panelists who appeared at the nine public Mandate events. It is their sage advice, based in many cases on years of service to the nation, that is being passed on to those who will serve in future administrations.

—Alvin S. Felzenberg

Introduction

Americans have a great stake in the transition of power from one President to the next. Even those who did not vote for the winning candidate should want the newly elected President of the United States to succeed in general. When the White House operates smoothly and the President is seen as a success, every American benefits. When the White House is in chaos and the President fails, they suffer.

Examples abound of Presidents who were unable to "hit the ground running" because of mistakes they made during the transition period. Richard Nixon and Jimmy Carter, for example, made early decisions to give their Cabinet secretaries primary authority over appointments to key policymaking posts within their departments. In practice, this decision meant their administrations similarly were unable to speak with a single voice in key policy areas. Confusion and even conflict resulted.

Bill Clinton declared early that he wanted his Cabinet to "look like America" and a woman to serve as Attorney General. These decisions led to speedy but sloppy, screening of the potential candidates and resulted in a series of rapid-fire embarrassments. The misguided effort known as "Nannygate" was not President Clinton's only early problem. One week after his election, he unexpectedly provoked controversy with a surprise promise to lift the ban on homosexuals serving openly in the military. Combined with the abrupt dismissal of veteran personnel from the White House Travel Office, the "growing pains" of the early months of the Clinton Administration produced months of backpedaling and, in the case of Travelgate, years of investigation, criticism, court battles, and conflict. For a while it seemed as though the new Chief Executive from Hope, Arkansas, would never recover.

Ronald Reagan, by comparison, strode into office insouciant and self-confident because he had a vision and clear plans for his Administration. Thanks to advance planning with a handful of his key advisers, Reagan entered the White House knowing exactly how his team would fill the key posts, how they would instruct their principal appointees, which positions would be filled and in what order, and which policies his Administration would push first.

Each of Reagan's three visits to Washington during the transition period furthered a specific objective. First, he met with the outgoing President; then he toured his future living quarters; and finally, he familiarized himself with important players in what distinguished historian Richard Neustadt calls the "Washington community." This community included the very people who would be working—and at times fighting—with key administration staff. By Inauguration Day on January 20, Reagan was ready. Just as important, to the American people and the media he *appeared* ready. Analysts of all political persuasions attribute the successes he enjoyed in the opening months of his presidency to these early steps, and they often cite his transition as a model for future Presidents to follow.

Traditionally, the peaceful transfer of power from one President to another after an election is a time of great expectation. The inauguration of the President of the United States, and especially the inauguration of a new President, with all its pageantry and solemnity has become a national ritual. President John F. Kennedy rightly called it a "celebration of freedom." To those still bereft of the blessings of democracy in other parts of the world, the inauguration of the American President, in public view and before his supporters and former opponents, continues to demonstrate the greatness of America.

The 70 days between the election and the swearing-in can be heady times for the President-elect and his team. They can also be chaotic. After a long and hard-fought campaign, veterans of the effort experience both the euphoria and the exhaustion that accompany victory. Often they display an understandable hubris, believing perhaps that nothing that awaits them can be as difficult or as arduous as what they have already achieved. Historians and journalists believe this arrogance was one of the underlying causes of Kennedy's miscalculation in the Bay of Pigs incident and prompted Clinton's ill-conceived economic stimulus package and health care proposal.

The days and weeks immediately after the long campaign—when people are tired, stressed, ecstatic, and more than a bit confused about what lies ahead—are not the best time for a President-elect and his closest advisers to make decisions that will affect the country and world for years to come. Yet, in an atmosphere conducive to error, they must make many such decisions and in quick succession. Presidents who either delay decisions on critical matters or act in haste will be sowing the seeds of future frustration.

Richard Nixon, for instance, who was unsure in the final weeks of his campaign that he would be elected, had a slow and awkward start to his Administration. Jimmy Carter planned for the transition, but much of this planning was done in a vacuum only to be unearthed after the election, when the campaign staff—

upset that they had not been consulted—began to focus on the transition.

Sometimes Presidents handicap themselves by placing a premium on fulfilling the promises of government "reform" they made during the heat of the campaign. Clinton, for example, pledged to reduce the size of the White House staff. Mindful that the press would be keeping count, members of his team often made cuts they later regretted.

To help the next American President prepare for a successful transition, The Heritage Foundation brought together alumni and observers of nine presidential administrations—spanning a period of nearly 50 years—for a series of discussions about what went right and what went wrong during transition periods and administrations past. More than 60 panelists and presenters participated in nine public forums that Heritage hosted in Washington during the fall of 1999 and spring of 2000. Among those who so generously shared their time and advice on the panels are: Theodore C. Sorensen, Counsel and key adviser to John F. Kennedy; veteran Washington journalists Michael Barone, Bob Franken, Michael Novak, Sander Vanocur, and Al Aisele; Leon Panetta, Bill Clinton's second Chief of Staff; Edwin Meese III, long-time Counsellor to Ronald Reagan and head of the Reagan transition team; Caspar Weinberger, Ronald Reagan's Secretary of Defense; Zbigniew Brzezinski, National Security Adviser to Jimmy Carter; Michael Deaver, Deputy Chief of Staff to Ronald Reagan; Tony Blankley, Press Secretary to House Speaker Newt Gingrich; Martin Anderson, Assistant to Ronald Reagan for Policy Development; Jack Watson, Jimmy Carter's Chief of Staff; C. Boyden Gray, Counsel to George Bush; Jack Valenti, Special Assistant to Lyndon B. Johnson; Directors of the White House Office of Presidential Personnel under Presidents Carter, Reagan, Bush, and Clinton; as well as political scientists Richard E. Neustadt, James Pfiffner, Paul Light, James Thurber, Martha Kumar, Shirley Anne Warshaw, Susan Tolchin, Colin Campbell, Stephen Hess, John Burke, and Robert Maranto.

The fruit of these forums and other activities are presented here. In sum, they can be summarized as eight keys to a successful presidency. They are offered in the general order that the next President and his transition team are most likely to pursue in structuring the executive branch and establishing a policy agenda. Each chapter addresses different types of questions that a new President must face, and the key steps he should take to answer them effectively.

1. **Achieving a Successful Transition:** What needs to be done? When, where, and by whom should each step be implemented?

2. **Running the White House:** How should the White House be organized? What system can be put in place to efficiently

handle the steady flow of people and paper? Who should have access to what? Who should have what authority?

3. **Staffing a New Administration:** How do you find the best people for the key positions? For that matter, how do you determine what the "best" is? What priorities should be set by filling the key posts? What management system will assure the President that the administration will further his own goals?

4. **Turning the President's Agenda into Administration Policy:** How will the White House interface with Cabinet departments and independent agencies? Where should policy be made?

5. **Enacting a National Security Agenda:** What vision does the President have for America's role in the world? What criteria should be used to select a National Security Adviser? How should the President, the National Security Adviser, Secretary of State, and Secretary of Defense interact?

6. **Working with Congress to Enact an Agenda:** How can the President ensure a desired program will become law? How do you facilitate smooth inter-branch relations?

7. **Managing the Largest Corporation in the World:** What are the President's primary managerial duties? How can the President ensure that his directives flow through the entire federal bureaucracy?

8. **Building Public Support for the President's Agenda:** How is a message developed, transmitted, and used to reinforce support among principal actors?

Heritage called on many experts—people who have "been there and done that," for better or for worse—to offer their advice to the next President and his administration. Although they sometimes disagreed in what to emphasize, most agreed on substance and the fundamentals of what a President should do.

For example, the panelists agreed that it is never too early for a presidential candidate to begin transition planning. He should designate a single individual to quietly undertake the arduous task of putting together the architecture to effectively transfer power from the current administration to the new one. This person must be somebody who has worked closely with the President in the past and who enjoys his full trust and confidence, and who understands the importance of people in implementing policy. Preferably, it is someone who also has connections in the Washington community.

Though some consider transition planning to be a modern phenomenon, Presidents have engaged in it since the days of George Washington. Rather than a sign of overconfidence or bravado, transition teams are a necessary management tool that spell the difference between success and failure in the first days of the new administration. Yet, among modern Presidents, only Ronald

Reagan had the foresight to begin planning early. Many others, in retrospect, undoubtedly wish they had.

One piece of advice often repeated at the Mandate for Leadership 2000 forums was the importance of paying attention to those minor details that, if ignored or handled badly, could cause serious heartburn for some time. Tom Korologos, who handled Senate relations for Richard Nixon and Gerald Ford, noted for example that "the big things kind of take care of themselves. Those little things kill you." One "little thing" that took on an importance far beyond anyone's expectations was a refusal by one of Carter's senior aides to give Speaker of the House Thomas P. "Tip" O'Neill additional inaugural tickets at his request. Washington insiders still regale in recalling that O'Neill, for the next four years, referred to the aide, Hamilton Jordan, as "Hannibal Jerkin."

As Leon Panetta observed, "lessons which are so obvious in this town [Washington] are never learned and everybody has to kind of reinvent the wheel." Incoming administrations tend to repeat the mistakes of past administrations because they lack the institutional memory that provides continuity to corporations, universities, and other great institutions during leadership changes. *The purpose of this volume is to provide that institutional memory, to give the next President of the United States practical advice on how to achieve success.* There are no silver bullets or magic pills in this book—only the accumulated wisdom of dozens of Washington veterans who have the ribbons and battle scars to prove it.

History shows that Americans benefit when presidential transitions run smoothly. When a new President is able to articulate clearly his vision for America; when the White House and Congress establish a good working relationship, even if they disagree on legislative and policy details; when the right people are selected for the right administration jobs; and when the President's team understands his priorities and has a plan for doing "first things first," then every American will profit.

This book is about success and failure, not policy or politics. We hope the wisdom gleaned from the experience of those who have walked the Pennsylvania Avenue walk will help the next U.S. President to avoid the kinds of unnecessary mistakes that have plagued past administrations, and we wish him every success.

—Alvin S. Felzenberg

Alvin S. Felzenberg is a Visiting Fellow at The Heritage Foundation and directs the Foundation's Mandate for Leadership 2000 Project. He writes, lectures, and comments regularly on the American presidency. He has held senior level positions in the Bush Administration and on Capitol Hill and served as New Jersey's Assistant Secretary of State. Dr. Felzenberg received his Ph.D. in Politics from Princeton University and has lectured on the presidency there and at other institutions.

PARTICIPANTS

Achieving a Successful Transition
May 31, 2000
St. Regis Hotel
Washington, D.C.

PHIL TRULUCK
Executive Vice President, The Heritage Foundation

Presenters

C. BOYDEN GRAY
Former Counsel to President George Bush

THE HONORABLE EDWIN MEESE III
Former Counsellor, President Ronald Reagan

THEODORE C. SORENSEN
Former Counsel to President John F. Kennedy

JACK VALENTI˙
Former Special Assistant to President Lyndon Johnson

JACK WATSON,
Former Chief of Staff to President Jimmy Carter

Commentators

JOHN BURKE
Professor of Politics, University of Vermont

MARTHA KUMAR
Professor of Political Science, Towson University

RICHARD E. NEUSTADT
Professor Emeritus, Harvard University

Chapter I:
Achieving a
Successful Transition

"If people are going to learn about their jobs, they need to do that early, because once you get into the White House, it's like drinking from a fire hose, and you don't have the time to read anything, to talk to people."
—Martha Kumar

From the time George Washington graciously made way for John Adams, the transfer of power from one American President to another has come to symbolize peaceful changes from one government to another. Be they smooth or tempestuous, transfers of power have showcased the best of American democracy to the world and demonstrated the virtues of self-government to people living under dictatorships.

In the post–World War II era, outgoing and incoming administrations have shown an increased awareness of this symbolism. Ever since the height of the Cold War, both sides have taken pains to show public signs of cooperation. After each election, the public has come to expect news accounts detailing who each side has placed in charge of its transition efforts and the obligatory "photo-op" of Presidents and Presidents-elect exchanging pleasantries.

Beyond the symbolism, the transition is a critical period for a President-elect. The decisions and public statements made during this period can have lasting effects on the new administration as Presidents-elect give form and substance to their administrations. Although the transition is said to begin immediately after the election, it actually begins before the election and runs well into the first year of a presidency. Thus, while most presidential campaigns deny that they have begun to plan for the transfer of power in the event they are successful, many have. In fact, more successful Presidents have begun planning for the transfer of power months before their election.

Richard Neustadt, Jack Watson,
Ted Sorensen, and Ed Meese

Where transitions were once informal ad hoc operations, today they are multi-million dollar ventures. For the past several years, Congress has provided money and space to incoming and outgoing transition teams and directed the U.S. General Services Administration to finance transition teams. Presidents-elect have used some of these funds to pay for a staff, which consists primarily of veterans from the campaign waiting for new assignments in the new administration, and to assess the state of the enterprise they will be inheriting.

Theodore C. Sorensen, who participated in President-elect John F. Kennedy's transition, observed that modern day transitions have evolved into a "cottage industry." He questions whether these now-institutionalized mechanisms are actually necessary:

> In the ten weeks they have as President-elect, new Presidents must decide questions ranging from personnel, to organization, to policy. Many of those need to be made quickly. Almost instantly after learning that he has been elected, the successful candidate must be ready to announce who they wish to direct the transition effort, who they will entrust to speak on their behalf throughout the process, and where he intends to spend most of his time prior to his election. Veterans of past transitions maintain that Washington is hardly the optimal place because of the intensive press scrutiny of their comings and goings and the importance of allowing the outgoing administration to continue to govern.

It is also during this period that Presidents must decide how they wish to organize the White House and which of their aides they wish to have working there. As argued in Chapter 2, most Presidents spend too much time selecting their Cabinet. Instead, Presidents should devote time to deciding who should serve in their inner circle and what qualifications are necessary for their close personal advisers.

Several hasty or ill-considered policy decisions made during a transition can have ramifications that affect the course of a presidency for years. For example, the Bay of Pigs operation under Kennedy, Carter's ill-fated energy proposals, and Clinton's experiences with gays in the military and health care reform all had their origins in poorly planned or executed transitions.

PLANNING DURING THE CAMPAIGN

A candidate is usually loath to plan for his presidency during the campaign, both for fear of tempting Providence and, more immediately, for fear of leaks to the press. Yet staff involved in transitions over the past 40 years, as well as scholars of the presidency, are unanimous in urging candidates to plan early for the possibility that they might win. The transition is a unique and valuable period for the incoming team, says Towson University Professor of Political Science Martha Kumar, and, accordingly, it calls for serious and early planning:

> Transitions do make a difference. There is a time period there that's different. There's a suspension of partisanship that exists that a new team can make use of. The difficulty is, it's a time when you have the greatest opportunity to do something but you have the least ability to make use of it, because you don't have the knowledge that you will have a couple of years into an administration.

> But in order to take advantage of that suspension of partisanship and move early, what you have to do is plan early. And plan early is bringing together information on possible people who could come into an administration, what kind of process you're going to use to consider nominees, and to consider what kinds of policy initiatives you're going to have as well, and also what your priorities can be. In order to pull that together successfully, it has to be done early.

Jimmy Carter's transition process effectively began on May 11 of the election year, when senior campaign aide Jack Watson wrote a memo to Carter recommending that he establish a small, confidential group:

> It was a memorandum that basically said, "Mr. President, unlike so many of the Presidents who have come into the White House, certainly in this century, you have had no federal government experience, save that in the United States Navy. You don't have a Washington network. You are the governor"—or former governor at that time—"of a southern state. You've not been a national figure before you entered the presidential primaries in New Hampshire and Iowa caucuses. I think it would be a good idea quietly to pull together, separate from the

campaign, a small group of people who would begin in the lowest-profile way possible, quietest most controlled way possible, to start gathering certain information and facts, putting that information and those facts, those recommendations together so that when and if you are elected President in November, you can commence the transition with something of a head start."

Watson followed up with other memos outlining his thoughts. As soon as Carter received the nomination on June 10, he instructed Watson to go ahead with his plan. By the time of the presidential election, Watson had a group working 14-hour days, seven days a week, essentially developing a checklist for Carter in the event he should win. Watson's final pre-election memo, sent to Carter on November 3, contained specific steps for the transition. Watson paraphrases the memo as follows:

"Mr. President, the day after the election, you are the President-elect, and you've got roughly 10 weeks within which time you must essentially organize your government, your administration, set certain priorities, start to form what will be your administration.

"Initiate telephone calls of appreciation to key people, both in the Congress and otherwise across the country, leaders who have helped you in one way or another to be elected. Set up a group to supervise responses to telegrams from foreign leaders. Meet with leaders of the campaign to confirm arrangements for closing the campaign down. Assign authority to a very limited number of people, with staff aides to manage the transition," and I suggested a transition coordinator, a director of the transition, and a press secretary, followed shortly thereafter by congressional liaison, as principal transition aides.

"Consider where you're going to be, Governor. Are you going to stay in Plains? Are you going to spend part of your time each week in Washington? How do you want to do that, because how you do that will both affect the way the matters in the transition are handled and will also project certain messages to the country."

Also, "Determine what you want the Vice President to do during the transition. Talk to Senator [Walter] Mondale, both for the purpose of getting his advice—Senator Mondale's been in Washington awhile—on a wide range of subjects, and collaboratively between the two of you, set out what you expect him to do during the transition, how to help, so forth and so on."

There is more, but that's what I mean when I say simple organizational checklists.

This practical, nuts-and-bolts approach must continue as the new President actually takes over. It is easy for a new President to forget such practicalities, points out Harvard University Professor of Government Richard Neustadt, when making commitments to run an efficient administration:

> If you must economize, or must symbolize economy, eliminate jobs for policy wonks and even, if Boyden Gray will allow me, lawyers—not good first-rate clerical people and messengers and what we used to call writing pages. The Carter Administration got rid of so many people at the lower but critical level that they couldn't even get their messages to the Hill delivered properly because they fired half the messengers. There are plenty of policy people whose jobs you could scrap and then restore them one by one as you need them. Don't fire the really important help, the secretaries and the messengers.

Ronald Reagan's transition also began with a small, secretive group meeting regularly before the election. Edwin Meese, who headed Reagan's transition team, explains the importance of this early planning:

> We had a small group of people who didn't have any particular contribution they could make to the campaign, in an office that was totally separate from the campaign headquarters—as a matter of fact, it was one city away—in absolute secrecy do the planning for the personnel operation. We realized that once the transition started, recognizing the very short period of time—I think we had 77 days—the one thing that you had to be prepared to do was to have a plan for handling personnel, and also to have a pretty good picture of what jobs had to be filled. So we had three or four people that were working on that.

THE PRESIDENT-ELECT'S ROLE

As senior Kennedy aide Ted Sorensen says, it is vital for the President-elect to recognize that the day after the election, he takes on a different role from that of candidate or that of President. Says Sorensen:

> Remember you are not now a candidate. Forget this business about the permanent campaign, the White House staffed primarily with former campaign workers who have no substantive policy experience, who are working up a daily message for the press and focusing on the 15-second sound bite for that

night's television—and still attacking the opposition
and scrambling for daily headlines and shunning the
incumbent.

And now it's not enough to give a great speech, or to
raise a profound question, or to point with alarm to
some oncoming peril. From now on, that's not
enough. You have to have answers. You have to run
the show, and from now on, every word you speak
is spoken to multiple audiences all around the country and all around the world, and you must exercise
much greater caution and provide much greater
depth when you speak. Your obligation now is not
merely to your party, but to all Americans.

Setting the Right Tone

Indeed, says Neustadt, it is important that the President-elect
understand that between the election and Inauguration Day, the
public is watching the candidate become the President. How the
President-elect undertakes this change will be of lasting importance:

Mr. Kennedy did it. Mr. Reagan did it, very carefully
and well—the public is very interested in watching
the candidate become President, if indeed they can
tell the difference. If they tell the difference, it makes
a lasting impression. The public relations ... of making that transition in perception is highly important,
because there's not going to be another time when
public attention is so focused on first impressions of
the new President as in the period December–January–February. There's no overemphasizing the
importance of looking different, looking presidential.

In particular, the President-elect must be careful not to complicate matters for the incumbent President. As Sorensen reminds
the next President-elect:

Mr. President-elect, remember you are not yet President. We only have one President at a time in this
country, and it's very important that during the next
several weeks you do nothing and say nothing that
will undermine the incumbent President and con-
fuse the world as to who is in charge. So you should
be careful what you say, and you should be careful
who has the right to speak for you—who is permit-
ted, even, to talk on your behalf, to government
leaders and so on around the world.

During this time you should not seek to advise the
incumbent President, either privately or publicly.
You should not endorse what his plans are, much

less attack what his plans are, even though many of them are long-range and going to affect you and perhaps impair your discretion in the White House. If he wishes to consult you in private on one of those long-term policies affecting your future, all right, but you still have the right to accept or reject, and he still has the right to accept or reject your advice.

Sorensen notes only one exception to this "hands-off" approach to the incumbent:

There is one exception, and that is on personnel matters. You can, if you wish, ask the President of the United States to impose a freeze on federal branch employment, or a hold on additional nominations, or a halt to transferring people from political Schedule C positions into permanent civil service positions. That's your right, to make those requests; it's still his right to say "no."

Meese explains that this was a major reason Reagan kept well away from Washington, except for a few carefully planned trips:

One of the good reasons to have the President outside the city is to make sure that there is no interference or no perceived interference, or any conflict between the incoming President and the President who really is there, so we were very careful during that period of time to make no comments about the Iranian situation and do nothing that would interfere in any way with Warren Christopher and the others that were trying to get those hostages back. This principle of "one President at a time" is, I think, a very important one.

It is also important to keep the President-elect out of town, says Martha Kumar, simply to allow him to rest:

The campaign is grueling, and the beginning of the government is going to be grueling as well, so he does need to use that period to recharge his batteries. Reagan very successfully did that. He had a sense of going, from his work in the movie industry, from one project to another and knew how to do downtime and was able to do it. Clinton kept things going, and when he came into the White House, some people felt he came in tired.

Setting the right tone also means building the necessary bridges to ensure a smooth handover and a good start for the new administration. As the "outsider," Ronald Reagan took steps during the post-election period to establish a climate of cooperation with Washington. To reach out to the city's leaders, Reagan made three trips to Washington before Inauguration Day. The first was a social visit, to acquaint himself with the people with whom he

Jack Valenti

Ted Sorensen and Jack Valenti

would be working, and to visit with President Carter. The second was more businesslike. Reagan met with Carter alone for two-and-a-half hours for a briefing on the main issues that the new President would face. His third visit came about a week before Inauguration Day, when he had a series of policy meetings leading up to the Inauguration.

Avoiding Mistakes

A President-elect, says Ted Sorensen, will be champing at the bit. But he must avoid the temptation to go astray, and into trouble, by unveiling new but ill-considered policy initiatives:

> You should resist that temptation in these heady days to undertake something that your press adviser or campaign worker tells you would be a bold initiative to go it alone, show that you're willing to take high risks, because now you're a winner and nothing bad can happen. Everybody at this table can tell you something bad that happened in those first 100 days because they made the mistake of thinking that they had all the answers and could take that kind of risk. The world is a whole lot more complex when you're inside the White House looking out than it was before, when you were on the outside looking in.

Presidents can avoid such mistakes, says University of Vermont Professor of Politics John Burke, by heeding warnings from experts and seasoned politicians. For example, during Bill Clinton's transition, he ignored advice to proceed carefully with health care reform and set up a lumbering, secretive task force that added to his political problems. More notably, Clinton's transition was marred by the gays in the military fiasco that dominated media attention:

> Senator Sam Nunn back in August of 1992 heard about the proposal that Mr. Clinton had made, contacted Mr. Clinton, and warned him about the firestorm that would likely emerge if he went through with it. Again, it was not advice that President-elect Clinton chose to heed.

Such care, says Richard Neustadt, should also be applied to actions and initiatives taken by the new President before he has had time to fully understand the government:

> Try to avoid actions after January 20 that are doubly unfamiliar: unfamiliar to the President who doesn't grasp the character of the organizations that will have to carry the actions out (as Mr. Kennedy, I think, did not grasp the internals of the CIA or the Joint Chiefs of Staff before the Bay of Pigs) but also unfamiliar to the bureaucracies or the congressional committees that will have to act.

> The real key to the Bay of Pigs is that nothing on that scale had ever been done by the Central Intelligence Agency before. Somewhat the same thing can be said of the Bert Lance affair in 1977, when Office of Management and Budget Director-designate Bert Lance wanted to revise the terms of his Senate confirmation, something no Senate committee had been asked to do for a long, long time if ever. Try to avoid the doubly unfamiliar in that sense until you've been there long enough to have some idea of what you're doing.

Concentrating on Top Staff

The President-elect, during the interregnum, should concentrate on the key decisions he must make. He and his top staff must be absolutely determined to maintain focus. According to Jack Watson:

> A successful transition … involves a careful and a meticulous process of exclusion. Decide what is most important, most immediate, for the President and his forming team, his inchoate team, to be paying attention to. The pressures on a President and his inchoate staff about things that should be on his agenda are overwhelming. So one of the main disciplines that a good director of transition and others working with him or her should do is setting priorities.

Meese agrees and recommends two priorities:

> You have to be very disciplined in what it is that the President and the other members of the transition team are going to do, and the two main things that a President has to do during that time are, number one, select his management team, primarily his Cabinet and the members of the White House staff, and secondly, determine his policy agenda in the sense of setting his primary goals so that he knows what it

is and can articulate this from ... Inauguration Day on.

In every campaign speech, [Reagan] had always mentioned two primary objectives. One was the revitalization of the economy, and the second was rebuilding our national defenses. So it was pretty easy to recognize that those were going to be the primary policy goals of the administration and to work that into the planning during the transition.

Reagan spent his transition period "holed up" in California beyond the intense glare of the Washington press corps. He concentrated on the process of selecting top White House and Cabinet officials. Explains Meese:

With the President-elect in California, that was where the Cabinet selection process was taking place. I would go out from Washington every week, and we would have a meeting with the President, particularly in the early weeks. We also had some of his so-called Kitchen Cabinet, who would help him with the appointment process in California when he was governor some years before that. They also were asked to select and recommend to him three people for every Cabinet position, and then he whittled those down, had interviews with the potential Cabinet members he didn't know.

It was much easier to do that with him in California, because you didn't have this horrendous press attention. There was a lot of press out there, but it was much easier for him to have these interviews privately, without an awful lot of attention as to who was coming and going to his private home. The fact that he was out there enabled him to do the two things that I mentioned that were priorities; that is, decide on his management team, make these appointments, and also be working on his major policy priorities.

It is extremely important to select the key White House staff early, says Martha Kumar, and then to establish a cordial, businesslike relationship with the incumbent's staff. There is so much to learn by Inauguration Day, and there is virtually no time. As Kumar explains:

If people are going to learn about their jobs, they need to do that early, because once you get into the White House, it's like drinking from a fire hose, and you don't have the time to read anything, to talk to people. What you need to do is have that done early, before you come in. For that reason, it is particularly important that a White House staff is appointed, and is appointed as soon after the election as is possible.

The Reagan team, says Meese, also paid close attention to the manner in which Cabinet announcements would be made:

> We scheduled the announcement of Cabinet members in two or three different groups. The purpose of that was so we wouldn't have a lot of leaking, a lot of piecemeal announcements along the way, and when we did present the Cabinet in these different iterations of three or four, maybe five or six at a time, then the press—that was their first opportunity. They were warned not to talk to the press, even if the press had gotten some inkling that they might be appointed and were hounding them, and we had very good cooperation from the prospective Cabinet members, not to talk to the press and not to give any interviews, and the first interview that they had was when they were actually presented to the press in a more formal setting.

In addition, Neustadt believes it is important that Cabinet nominees understand that their role is not to be the President's close advisers; instead, they are to carry out tasks that are much more down-to-earth:

> The President must prepare the Cabinet members against the shocking discovery that most of them are not the principal advisers to the President, and are not going to be, and never will be, not since the White House staff has come into a mature existence. Most of them won't understand that as they go in, and most Presidents-elect won't understand it either. If they go in with exaggerated ideas of their importance to the system, they will then discover that they have to front for their civil servants; they have to spend half their time on the Hill testifying; they have to deal with their congressional subcommittees. Their perspective will get farther and farther from the White House perspective, and the result will be considerable unhappiness for most of them.

Moreover, says John Burke, the President-elect must be clear in his own mind as to the roles of the top White House and Cabinet officials. These roles will have a profound impact on how the President should organize his White House and administration:

> It's important to consider how these individuals who are appointed to the White House staff fit together in a decision-making process that will come to bear once the President is in office. Here I think there's an interesting contrast between the Carter transition and, again, the Reagan transition.
>
> Jimmy Carter wanted Cabinet government. He spoke frequently about Cabinet government, thought about the Cabinet as having a very central

role within his policymaking, yet little was done during the transition to bring this to fruition. It was a piece of the transition that dropped out of the way.

In 1980, it was quite different. Ronald Reagan, coming from his practice as Governor of California, was interested in continuing that practice of bringing the Cabinet centrally into his decision-making, but there was also a realization that change needed to be made, that there had to be some adaptation to the realities of Washington, to the larger number of federal departments and so on. So through the transition period, as everything else was going on, as the Cabinet was being appointed, there was also a very constructive dialogue, a very constructive process of deliberation to try to figure out, how can we make Cabinet government work in a way that would fit with the realities that will come to bear after Inauguration Day?

This led to the Cabinet Council system that Ed Meese and others developed.

THE TRANSITION PROCESS

Campaigning versus Governing

Campaigning and governing are very different, as many politicians have learned the hard way. A winning campaign staff may not be a winning team in the White House. Jack Watson recalls that he felt like a javelin catcher, not just as Carter's Chief of Staff, but as the transition chief:

> One of the biggest problems that we had, now well-known because it's been written about, was the merging of the campaign staffs and the transition teams, pulling together those people who had been devoting their lives on the road and otherwise to the election of Jimmy Carter as President in 1976 and those people who had been working equally hard in a more policy-oriented way, and in a more governance way, trying to get the President-elect ready for the transition of 1976 and merging those two operations, one very, very large campaign organization and this other small team, which in this case had been headed by me.

Experts and former officials disagree on the degree to which campaign staff should be placed within the new administration team. In her survey of former White House officials for the White House 2001 Project, Kumar has found them divided:

> There are a lot who feel that campaign people are inappropriate for a White House because the kind of

schedule ... they're working on is day-to-day. They're not doing anything long-range. They tend to be working on an image of their guy as good, the other guy is bad, and attack; and when you come into a White House, you need a very different kind of person, one that can work over time, people who compromise.

Also, people who tend to come in from the campaign, as Dick Neustadt has observed, can be characterized sometimes by their arrogance, ignorance, and adrenaline, and they're difficult to rein in.

On the other hand, there are people that say it is important to have campaign people because they know the rhythms of a President. It's important to have an understanding of what his needs are, what he likes, how he likes to get his information. Does he want to get it on paper? Does he like to get it verbally? Is he a morning person? An afternoon person? All of that you need to know right at the start, and it's the campaign people that know that.

Campaign people are people who are battle-tested. They can work on deadlines, so you don't have to find that out in a White House. And, importantly, they have the campaign memory. They are the institutional memory. They have a sense of why they're there. And when those people leave a White House, that White House can sometimes be in trouble and the administration lose its course. There are those who have felt, in the Reagan Administration, that Iran–Contra came about partially because those campaign people were no longer in the White House.

Similarly, senior officials and advisers to recent Presidents have a range of views on this subject. Lyndon Johnson's aide, Jack Valenti, for example, feels it is necessary for a President to surround himself with people who have been "under fire," particularly people from his campaign:

I think a President must have around him in the White House people that he trusts, and the only people you know you trust are the people who you've known in the past, who have taken bullets in their stomach for you and keep going. I would not have anybody on my staff, frankly, if I were President that I really didn't know well. How is he going to perform when the dagger is at the belly? You don't know until you have seen this fellow in action.

Others, like Ted Sorensen, take a somewhat different view. Sorensen accepts that it is important for a President to bring in the people he has grown to trust over many years, including those who worked in his campaign. However, he notes, it is critical that the President ensure that he draws upon people who have substantial experience in government.

Guidelines for a Transition Team

Just as the President-elect should focus on the most important decisions, John Burke argues that the transition effort itself must not be too all-encompassing if it is to be successful:

> There is one paradox that I think has occurred when you look at the last four transitions. Two of the transitions were quite ambitious in the pre-election period: those in 1976 under Mr. Carter and Mr. Watson and then more recently in 1992 under Mickey Kantor during the Clinton transition. The other two, the Reagan transition of 1980 and the Bush transition of 1988, had much more limited mandates, and yet I would argue that they tended to be more successful in terms of the transition that occurred after the election as well as in the governing period.

The Reagan transition team was particularly focused on coordination and on the end results it wanted. To avoid potentially damaging friction within the civil service, for example, Ronald Reagan's top aides were careful to define how the transition teams should operate and what the teams should do. As Ed Meese explains:

> We did send transition teams into all the departments and many of the agencies, but we gave them the mission not to be a conquering army coming in and taking over or harassing the people who were there, but rather to be information gatherers, because there's a lot that can be gathered and a lot that needs to be known, particularly for an administration like ours which is coming in very new with many people who had not had experience in the federal government before. Some had, among the Cabinet, but many had not.
>
> The briefing books that they provided as a result of their information gathering were extremely important to many of the department heads. Basically, these briefing books had such things as the organization of the department, the staff, the appointments that would have to be made in the early days, the major functions of the department, and a particular feature that we asked for, which was to ask the outgoing people in the departments, "What are the major problems that are going to be encountered in the first 90 days that the new Cabinet and the new members of that particular department, the assistant

secretaries and so on, are going to have to deal with?"

Meese also says that they were careful to make sure the activities of the transition teams and the President-elect's policy team were coordinated and they were speaking with the same voice:

> It was very important that there be coordination, so one of the things we did was to have a 7:30 meeting every morning of all the division heads where we could talk about what was happening, plan the activities for the next several days, develop an answer to the problems that inevitably come up, and basically make sure everybody was going in the same direction. I think the largest we got up to at any one time was a little over a thousand people doing something relating to either the inaugural or the transition. So this kind of coordination was very necessary.

Equally important was the use of the transition period as a time to develop a strategic plan for the first six months of the administration. Meese explains:

> If I had to say what was the unique contribution that our transition made to the history of transitions, it was the development of a strategic plan for the first 180 days of the presidency. We figured out that it was exactly six months between the 20th of January when the President was inaugurated and the middle of August when Congress traditionally took their summer recess, and it was that honeymoon period that was very critical for the President to get his program through Congress.

> With the tax rate reduction and some of the other economic steps, and with the budget relating to the military, this was going to be a major congressional effort. So we had one person, Dick Worthman, who was assigned to develop a strategic plan, to combine the policy recommendations, to schedule when appointments would be made and milestones and deadlines for appointments, to bring in the communications aspects, when there should be presidential speeches and so on so that we have a general outline of what ought to be done during that first 180 days.

> And that strategic plan then brought together the various aspects not only of the transition, but also the future aspects of the White House and the presidency itself and how you could integrate these various parts: What the role of Cabinet members would be, what the role of the various departments and the various sections in the White House would be, and also the people that had to be contacted, the liaisons

that had to be established in order to bring together the primary policy objectives and have them accomplished by the time of the congressional recess in August of 1981.

Developing Good Relations with the Press

Successful campaigns usually develop a good working relationship with the press, but once the election is over, they must establish a completely different relationship. The White House

Jack Valenti and Jack Watson

press corps is not the same as the campaign media, and it can be daunting for freshly appointed transition staffers to deal with the media onslaught. Carter transition chief Jack Watson recalls his "baptism by fire" just after the 1976 election:

We finished our initial meeting, made certain arrangements, certain agreements. Certain administrative details were attended to, and President Ford's Press Secretary, Ron Nessen, said, "Jack, the press is out front. Would you like to go out and say something to the press? They'd like very much to see you since you're the first Georgian to cross the Potomac. Or if you don't want to do that, I'll just take you out the side door of the West Wing, and you can be on your way."

And I said, "What do you suggest that I do?" And he said, "Well, I'd suggest that you go out and say something to the press." And I said, "Well, all right."

We came to the front door of the West Wing, and as we got to the door I saw a large, loud, raucous group of people that looked more like a mob than the White House press corps and leading this group was Sam Donaldson.

I can feel it even now, a little bit. My knees kind of buckled. I took my breath in before I walked out the front door of the West Wing, and as I did it, I approached this group of screaming folks. The press secretary who was at my arm and kind of holding me, leading me along, said simply, "Welcome to Washington, Jack."

To try to keep relationships with the press as smooth and coordinated as possible, the Reagan team set up a press section that talked to the press and gave them as much information as possible. If the President-elect is to get good press, says Neustadt, he must treat the White House press with great care and attention:

> I would try to cushion the White House press corps—especially its new members, because many people are newly assigned after the election—against the terrible frustrations of being thought by their own organizations to be important and being treated as important but actually living in semi-imprisonment. It's worthwhile to be quite tender with the White House press corps during the transition.

> Mr. Kennedy did this without even having to think about it. For one thing, he divided his time between Palm Beach, Manhattan, and occasionally Washington. The press loved to go to Manhattan, and they loved to go to Palm Beach. But can you imagine how they felt in Plains, Georgia, living in Americus at a cruddy hotel for weeks at a time and then having to go play softball with the President, who they claimed cheated on them?

> By January 20, the press just raged against Mr. Carter. So give them some people to talk to. Give them some news to distribute. Give them a sense of importance. It can be done. And give them nice places to take their wives at Christmas time. Terribly important.

Get to Know the FBI

It is critical for the success of an administration that the FBI clear the new President's nominees quickly to reduce the lengthy confirmation process. Edwin Meese urges the next President-elect's team to move swiftly on this:

> Get acquainted with the Director of the FBI rather rapidly and get his support and cooperation in the clearance investigations, the background investigations of your people, and also particularly important is to ask the FBI Director that if they come across a snag with anybody that they're investigating would he please let you, the Transition Director, know directly when that happens, that you would much prefer to find it out from him than through the pages of *The Washington Post* or *The Washington Times*.

An important factor during the pre-election period, says presidential scholar John Burke, is the degree of oversight provided by the campaign organization over personnel selection:

> One of the things that Ed Meese did while also directing the campaign and having a central role in it was to meet if not daily, almost daily with Pendleton James, who was directing the personnel selection operation during the pre-election phase.

President Bush's Counsel, Boyden Gray, also emphasizes the importance of making the earliest possible start on the clearance process—even if it is not clear what jobs the individual will be nominated for, if any.

> Start people through the FBI process the day after the election. Even if you don't know what jobs they're going to have, you will know that there are 100 or 150 people who will serve in key jobs, in the White House and in the departments, and start them right away.... Set up a good relationship with the Director of the FBI; that's the first thing you ought to do. In fact, that ought to have been done before the election. But you cannot waste November, December, and January for the clearance process, because there will be a bottleneck and inevitably things will slow down. You cannot waste those months; you cannot waste any day.

Doing this, he adds, also increases the chances of avoiding the kind of embarrassment that followed the nomination of John Tower. Gray says one of his irritations as President Bush's incoming Counsel was getting the transition team to provide the names of candidates:

> After we got into the White House, things were slow. I kept begging the transition team for names. I said, "I don't care what jobs they have. Just let me start them." They wouldn't do it.

Making the clearance system move quickly, says Gray, also reduces the opportunity for Congress to add to the difficulties:

> If the Hill gets in on the act, and if you don't have your nominees ready to go before the legislative process starts to begin, they use nominees as hostages to get their programmatic preferences. Democrats as well as Republicans do this, even with nominees of their own party. If you're not done and ready to go with a substantial number of people, people being policy, you will get tripped up the way President Clinton was in the beginning. You have to run these checks before you announce the people.

PARTICIPANTS

Running the White House
November 18, 1999
St. Regis Hotel
Washington, D.C.

PHIL TRULUCK
Executive Vice President, The Heritage Foundation

Presenters

THE HONORABLE EDWIN MEESE III
Former Counsellor, President Ronald Reagan
THE HONORABLE LEON PANETTA
Former Chief of Staff to President William J. Clinton

Commentators

MICHAEL BARONE
Senior Writer, U.S. News & World Report
JOHN HARRIS
White House Correspondent, The Washington Post
STEPHEN HESS
Senior Fellow in Government Studies,
The Brookings Institution
KELLY D. JOHNSTON
Former Secretary of the United States Senate, 104th Congress
MARTHA KUMAR
Professor of Political Science, Towson University
JAMES P. PFIFFNER
Professor of Government and Public Policy,
George Mason University
ALEXIS SIMENDINGER
White House Correspondent, National Journal
GEORGIA SORENSON
James MacGregor Burns Academy of Leadership,
University of Maryland
JAMES A. THURBER
Center for Congressional and Presidential Studies,
American University
KAREN TUMULTY
White House Correspondent, Time Magazine

Chapter II:
Running the White House

*"[It's] important to establish rules regarding discipline,
behavior, and access to the President, to briefings,
to events, to Air Force One."*

Leon Panetta

Early in his term, a new President must make a series of important decisions, including designating his principal aides and
determining the structure of his administration that includes the
400 to 500 members of the White House staff as well as 1,200 to
1,300 staff members housed in the Executive Office of the President.

Usually the most important decision a President-elect will make
is his choice of Chief of Staff, a position of recent vintage, to oversee this large organization. In practice, the Presidents have tried
different organizational structures to run the White House effectively. These different structures offer lessons to any new President.

The nation's earliest Presidents managed with one or two assistants, chiefly to handle correspondence. Presidents conducted
their own negotiations with Congress and directed government
business through the Cabinet. Presidential assistants, few as they
were, stayed in the background.

For the last half century, however, almost every President has
designated one principal adviser to organize and supervise the
rest of the White House staff. The need for such a post arose from
the increase in size of the President's staff and the bureaucracies
that emerged as institutional appendages to it the middle of the
20th century. While some Presidents tried to manage without a
chief of staff, all found it necessary to designate a trusted person
to oversee the President's schedule; direct the flow of paperwork,
information, and people to and from the Oval Office; provide the
President with multiple policy options; present the President and
his message in the best possible light; adjudicate budgetary and
turf disputes between Cabinet officers; and "take the heat" for
unpopular decisions.

Ed Meese

The more recent Presidents all appointed a chief of staff, although the appointees varied greatly in style and in the authority they wielded. Students of the presidency regard the methods of operation adopted by Ronald Reagan during his first term and Bill Clinton from July 1994 through January 1997 as those most conducive to achieving a President's goals.

The systems used by Reagan and Clinton differ in one important respect. Reagan, in his first term, chose a "troika" of three trusted advisers to be at the helm of his White House operation: James A. Baker, Edwin Meese, and Michael Deaver. Clinton chose Leon Panetta, a strong but widely respected chief of staff reminiscent of Ford's choice of Richard Cheney.

Although the duties of Reagan's principal aides varied, with Meese responsible for policy, Deaver for the President's image, and Baker for paper flow, scheduling, and personnel, Baker was in many ways a traditional chief of staff. And although Panetta's primacy in Clinton's White House was apparent, he depended heavily on two deputies: Clinton loyalists Harold Ickes and Erskine Bowles.

Academic and political observers credit the success of the Reagan and Clinton presidencies, particularly during the Baker-Meese-Deaver period and the Panetta era, to how Reagan and Clinton chose to organize White House operations.

THE CHANGING NATURE OF THE PRESIDENCY

It was once customary for political science texts to describe the American President as the wearer of many "hats": chief executive, commander in chief, chief legislator, chief diplomat, head of state, leader of his party. Recent studies sometimes add manager of the economy. Yet Presidents do not wear one hat at a time; they often have to wear several simultaneously. In the past 50 years, the increase in the powers of the federal government and the centralization of policy development within the presidency have stretched the size of these hats. Furthermore, changes in technology, society, and the economy have added new responsibilities to the presidency.

As former Clinton Chief of Staff Leon Panetta observes, the demands on the presidency today are enormous and often contradictory.

> The President [today] is not only commander in chief. He is also the chief negotiator, ambassador, and diplomat to the world. He is the primary policymaker that can have an impact on issues from the economy to budget to health care to other domestic areas. He is clearly the key spokesperson not only for his administration, but for the nation as well, in charge of a modern bully pulpit that has increased its impact with the expansion of television, the Internet, and all of the other high tech communications networks that are so much part of our society.
>
> He is head of the political party. And our demands are that he raise huge amounts of money, not only for himself, but also for the party and for members and candidates of that party. He is largely in charge of relations with the leadership and members of the Congress. He has to often deal with the members of both the Senate and the House.
>
> He has to be the national chaplain. He has to calm and console and often care for the victims of crises and disasters. He is the host to countless visiting dignitaries and officials and friends and visitors to the White House. He is the leader of an administration and responsible for what goes on in the various Cabinet departments and agencies in the federal government. He is husband. He is father. He's America's first citizen and the constant focus of rumor and scandal and jokes and tabloid stories and political attacks. Other than that, it's not a bad job.

The many roles performed by today's President, Panetta explains, have changed the nature of the presidency and the White House support system needed to staff the presidency:

> The role of the staff has gone from being largely a liaison or conduit to the Cabinet and to other officials to being now a central policy coordinator and indeed, policymaker. In a very fast-moving world in the presidency, proximity is power. And if that's the case—and I believe it is—then obviously staff in the closest proximity to the President can have the greatest degree of power in influencing the decisions of that President.

Still, the new President can put his own stamp on the structure of the White House, and he can choose how he interacts with the Cabinet and the White House staff. Reagan Counsel Edwin Meese points out from his experiences that the new President has complete authority to decide how to organize and staff the White House. He starts with a clean slate:

> How the White House runs is, to a great extent, a reflection of the personality and the style of each President. It reflects in many ways the political interests and also the policy objectives of the President. For example, when President Reagan's Administration came into office, we found that the Carter Administration had several positions and several units that were different from those which followed in our Administration. This had to do with the particular objectives and interests of the respective Presidents.
>
> In one sense, each President and his staff, when they take the White House over, come in and start from scratch. I remember arriving on the afternoon of the 20th of January 1981, after the big parade and all the ceremonies were over. I found desk drawers absolutely empty—I think there was one paper clip—and filing cabinets with no documents in them.

On the other hand, notes George Mason University Professor of Government James Pfiffner, there may be less to this freedom than there first appears:

> The President of the 21st century is no longer free to do some of the things that early Presidents could do. Whoever takes office in 2001 is not free to do a number of things. He or she is not free to have a leisurely transition. He or she is not free to implement Cabinet government.
>
> It is not possible to run the administration without an assertive White House staff and, I would argue, not possible to run the White House without a chief of staff. It's not possible to choose personally most of the people who will be appointed in the administration. It's not possible to present a broad and varied policy agenda to Congress. At least, if a President ignores these lessons of recent presidencies there are going to be significant problems.

A new President may also find it difficult to focus on the task of building the staff that will be closest to him on a daily basis. As Brookings Institution scholar Stephen Hess points out:

> [Presidents] have to be concerned with the rate of inflation, with the rate of employment, with whether we are at war or peace. All of these things change over time and his needs change in that regard, too. The problem in part is that Presidents don't particularly think about [the White House structure]. They

have much more important things to think about than organization and personnel. They start in a transition, in the period between their election and their inauguration, and they are overwhelmed with questions of personnel. They design an organizational chart and they never again think about it as intensely as they do early on (unless something quite dysfunctional happens, as I think happened in the early Clinton Administration for a variety of reasons).

They look on it as almost a butterfly that you can pin to a corkboard—you can come back and look at it and see its beauty and it's always the same.

THE ROLE OF THE CABINET

While centralization of power and policy development are likely to remain in the White House, Cabinet departments and agencies continue to have the expertise, institutional memory, and skills necessary to implement them. They also are required by statute to discharge certain functions. Unlike White House aides, those who carry out these line functions are accountable to Congress and the public. Some Presidents have stumbled when they, or those with whom they had entrusted power, forgot this delineation of authority.

Dwight Eisenhower and Ronald Reagan took special steps to see that their cabinets and the White House functioned as a team, with all the players knowing their proper roles. Eisenhower would assemble everyone who had an interest in or responsibility for a certain area. Each attendee would then air before him the options available and their special "take" on a subject. Eisenhower would then decide the matter and rely on the White House staff to follow up to ensure that his wishes were carried out.

Reagan tried to meet a similar objective by meeting with smaller groups designated as "Cabinet Councils." (See Chapter 4.) He would occasionally meet with lower level officials to keep them apprised of administration policy. All of these efforts helped ensure that presidential appointees carried out the President's objectives rather than those of the departments or constituent groups. They also helped ensure that professionals implemented decisions.

Whenever there is a change of party in the presidency, incoming administrations assume the civil service will resist the new administration's initiatives. But administration veterans from both parties affirm that the professional service can be responsive to the President's policies if the relationship is carefully developed. Like political appointees, the professional service also needs to be apprised early of the President's objectives.

As Edwin Meese explains, Reagan believed that building a team based on the Cabinet was critically important to carrying out his mission:

> One of the things that President Reagan was very strong on, right from the start, was the involvement of the Cabinet and having the Cabinet as the principal forum for decisionmaking. He had developed that idea of the Cabinet in California during his governorship, and he carried it over into the White House.
>
> He was cognizant of the role that Henry Kissinger had played, for example, in the Nixon Administration, where in a sense he overshadowed the Secretary of State when he was the national security assistant. To some extent, Zbigniew Brzezinski had had a similar role under Carter. And there was a concern that the Cabinet not be in any way overshadowed by the White House staff and that the White House staff be seen in a subordinate role.

Meese also says that the direct involvement of the President was a key to achieving the right chemistry:

> When the President was in town, it was not at all unusual for him to participate in four to six Cabinet events every week. There would normally be a full Cabinet meeting at least once a week. He would then have Cabinet Council meetings, usually one or two of the councils related to domestic matters, and then two or three times a week with the National Security Council.
>
> This meant that the Cabinet members had frequent contact with the President in a formal setting, but also informally before and after Cabinet meetings. They had the sense that they were in close touch with what was going on in the White House and particularly, that they had the opportunity to be with the President on a regular basis.

BUILDING A TEAM AROUND THE PRESIDENT

The Reagan team recognized that many items are not suitable for discussion by the Cabinet as a whole but are best handled through subgroups, or Cabinet Councils, based on key members of the Cabinet and key White House staff. As Meese explains:

> [Reagan] created the Cabinet Councils, which was an innovation, although it was patterned after the one Cabinet Council that had been created by a statute in 1947: the National Security Council.

In the first term, President Reagan had eight Cabinet Councils: one for economic affairs, one for commerce and trade, another for agriculture and food policy. That was an interesting one. Why would a specific subject like that have a Cabinet Council all to itself? The reason was the grain embargo and the fact that agricultural policy pertained to both domestic and foreign policy. So it was deemed necessary, at least for a couple of years, to have that council.

Then there was the council on legal policy, a council on management administration, a council on the environment and natural resources, and one on human services. In the second term, those were collapsed into three Cabinet Councils, the Economic Policy Council, the Domestic Policy Council, and the National Security Council.

Furthermore, Meese notes, Reagan recognized that it was important for the President to reach beyond the Cabinet itself to build a strong and united team throughout his Administration.

An important part of managing the government is team-building. That is for the President to keep in touch, even though it's very difficult to do, with not just the Cabinet members but with the sub-Cabinet members, the undersecretaries, the deputy secretaries, the assistant secretaries, all of whom are his appointees and who feel at the start a great loyalty to the President. And one of the purposes of the White House staff is to maintain that loyalty throughout the presidency.

During our Administration, we held meetings several times a year in the Indian Treaty Room or in the auditorium of the Old Executive Office Building at which these sub-Cabinet officials would hear talks by the President or by other Cabinet members, and as a result, continuing to feel that they were part of a team.

REACHING OUT TO THE CIVIL SERVICE

Experience shows that it is also vitally important for the President to make his objectives clear to the permanent civil service, especially when there is a change of party. As Leon Panetta notes:

If someone from another party gets elected, there's going to be a natural suspicion and paranoia about the career service, as to whether or not they're really going to represent the ideals of the new presidency. They've served under another party. They've

become ingrained with the other party's point of
view on issues and priorities.

This requires the new President to embark on a form of diplomatic offensive with the civil service. There are three specific reasons for this, says Meese, although he admits that not all the senior officials in the Reagan team followed through with the strategy:

> [First, a] President and his appointees, his Cabinet
> and subcabinet people, have to be clear in what their
> objectives are and provide that leadership so that the
> people in the career service know. Second, they
> have to provide actual leadership, knowing what
> their people are doing and being available for two-
> way conversation even when somebody says that's a
> dumb idea that was tried two administrations ago,
> and give respect to the civil service. And third, I
> think there are a lot of little things that people in
> government can do to show their respect for the
> career servants, like going to the award ceremonies
> that they have a couple of times a year. I was some-
> what appalled that only two or three of us out of the
> Cabinet would attend those things on a regular
> basis, supporting the Federal Executive Institute by
> going out there to lecture occasionally, and doing
> those kinds of things to let them know that you
> believe that career service is important.

THE CRITICAL ROLE OF THE WHITE HOUSE STAFF

David Broder and Ed Meese.

As the presidency plays an increasing role in policy development both within the executive branch and throughout the American political system, Presidents have come to rely on larger numbers of people to assist them. Presidents once conducted government affairs through Cabinet officers and handled legislative relations themselves. They relied on a handful of clerks to assist them with correspondence and other chores related to managing the President's official and private household.

In recent years, Presidents have had between 400 and 500 people on their personal staffs, and they oversee mini-bureaucracies numbering more than 1,000. Meese has observed that these presidential helpers usually fall into one of three categories: those who serve the President personally, those who develop policy or perform liaison or management functions, and those engaged in communications and other forms of "outreach."

In organizing the White House staff, Presidents have varied greatly in their style of operation. Some preferred loose structures, while others thought of themselves as the hub of a wheel with staff emanating from the center like spokes. Others prefer pyramid-like arrangements with the President at the top of a structured bureaucracy. Most experts agree, however, that in whatever direction a new President wishes to go, he must make this decision early—preferably even before he takes office.

The Executive Functions of White House Staff

Ed Meese says that there are three critical decisions that need to be made regarding the operations of the White House:

> In determining the organization and structure of the White House and the reporting relationships, there are three critical decisions that a President has to make. One has to do with access—who will have immediate access to him and who will have what you might call deferred access, or have to have authorization through one of the other higher level staff members. A President's time—his time and energy—are probably the most valuable commodities that he has. They have to be guarded carefully or the President will be inundated with people, all of whom have great ideas of what he ought to do or how he ought to do it.
>
> A second decision has to do with the paper flow and the approvals that are necessary. When someone calls a department of the government and says, "This is the White House calling," I've always felt the proper retort should be, "I don't speak to buildings." But nevertheless, when you say it's the White House calling, there is tremendous power behind those few words. So, it's important to establish a structure of paper flow and information flow, but also of authorization of who can say what or request what.
>
> And third, the President has to make a decision in regard to the role of the Cabinet. How will the Cabinet relate to him and how will it relate to the White House staff?

A President can address these questions in various ways, depending on what he feels will work best for him. But whatever approach is used, says Leon Panetta, it is important to appoint the senior staff as soon as the President is elected:

> That ought to be on a new President's schedule every bit as much as looking at a new Cabinet, because you need to have your personal team in place as you move forward. I would suggest the following: You need to have your chief of staff and your deputies if possible, because that's your key management operation in the White House. You need to have your key foreign policy team. The head of the NSC [National Security Council] is now largely responsible for coordinating all foreign policy issues with the State Department and the Defense Department playing their role. But make no mistake about it, the NSC Director is extremely important to the foreign policy development of the presidency.

> The same thing is true with the economic team and the Directors of the NEC [National Economic Council] and the OMB [Office of Management and Budget]. Those individuals ought to be appointed. They can be appointed as part of the economic team, but they ought to be appointed early. The Domestic Policy Council is important to coordinate other Cabinet members who are put in place to deal with domestic issues. You also need the White House Counsel, because of the legal issues that can take place and will take place in any administration; the press secretary and communications director because of the communications responsibility; and the legislative director.

> All of these key positions ought to be filled early so that when the President takes office, there is a team in place that can immediately respond to issues. There is a tendency to think that the honeymoon period of an administration will last for a long time and that there will always to be an opportunity to appoint this team. The reality is: If you are not establishing policy within the White House on Inauguration Day, if you are not taking the offensive within the White House, then others will. It's just the nature of this town.

The Size and Composition of the White House Staff

While making sure that the top positions are filled, the next President should ponder whether the number of White House staff in recent years has grown beyond the efficient level. As commentator Michael Barone notes, the White House was not always so large. Franklin D. Roosevelt won World War II with about a dozen staffers. But today, more than 1,000 people work within the Executive Office complex:

> I often wondered as I walked by the White House to the Old Executive Office Building, or as I went into the West Wing: What are all those people doing? I'm not sure that there's not a great amount of staff doing memos to staff and staff initiating things mainly to interface with other staff. And that staff may also be in the Cabinet departments. It may be in Congress, where staff are constantly dreaming up bills.
>
> I would recommend to the next administration that they at least think about whether or not they could function, at least initially, with somewhat less staff, and not take it as inevitable that you need the large number of people working there. Because once you get them in, you're not going to get rid of them. So you might at least start off with the leaner staff and see if you could do this.
>
> … If you go look through the telephone books, there are deputies and subdeputies and assistants to the subdeputy. And in fact, the title profusion in this administration has really gotten baroque and wonderful. I suspect that there are a number of people in this administration, as there have been others, who can't remember their own title.

According to Pfiffner, the modern President has to assert his authority over a huge, sprawling government, and this accounts for the growth of the President's staff. He further notes that in the 1960s, there were about 250 people in the White House office structure. By the 1970s, there were 575 in the Nixon Administration, and today there are slightly over 400 people. The White House staff has grown so substantially, he says, because many things that used to be done outside of the White House are now done inside:

> Most domestic policy used to be done in the departments and agencies. Now it's coordinated by the domestic policy staff in the White House. National security, which used to be handled by State, Defense, and the CIA, is now done by the National Security Council staff. Legal advice to the President used to given by the Attorney General and the Justice Department. Now there's a bunch of lawyers in the White House Counsel's office. Trade policy used to be done in State, Agriculture, Commerce, and so forth. Now the U.S. Trade Representative is in the Executive Office of the President.

> Things that used to be done by political parties are
> now done inside the White House. Personnel
> recruitment used to be done by political parties.
> Now there's the Office of Presidential Personnel.
> Congressional coalition-building on the Hill used to
> be dominated by political parties and now the Office
> of Congressional Liaison does that. Interest group
> outreach used to be done by political parties. Now
> the Office of Public Liaison in the White House does
> it. Political tactics and strategy used to be much
> more influenced by the Democratic National Com-
> mittee and the Republican National Committee, but
> are now in the Office of Political Affairs in the White
> House.

> So the new President in 2001 cannot easily jettison
> any one of these offices, I think. And so I predict
> that probably it's going to be hard to cut back seri-
> ously on the White House staff.

A small but significant part of the growth during the Clinton
Administration was due to the inclusion of political consultants
in key meetings. This pattern worries former Clinton Chief of
Staff Panetta:

> I think because of the message part of the presi-
> dency, there will be a growing reliance on pollsters
> and consultants to help fashion that message. And
> that's true not just in the White House, that's true
> throughout the world. The reality is that both par-
> ties now rely heavily on consultants and pollsters to
> kind of develop their "message."

> … There were times, frankly, when people like Dick
> Morris crossed that line, and I thought that is not
> something that should be taking place in the White
> House. Yes, you can check the pulse. Yes, check
> what's happening out there in terms of the polls. But
> when that line is crossed and suddenly the polls are
> telling you what kind of policies you want to imple-
> ment—I say that not only in the White House, but
> on Capitol Hill too—I think that's dangerous,
> because people do not elect their representatives to
> follow the advice and consultation of what a pollster
> says ought to be the policy of this country. That, I
> think is a very dangerous trend. I think future Presi-
> dents are going to have to be very careful that they
> don't cross the line.

THE ROLE OF THE CHIEF OF STAFF

Modern Presidents appear to have accepted the notion that
whatever their personal style of operation, they need to place a

trusted aide in charge of White House operations. Even those who have felt that they did not need a chief of staff when they came into office appointed one. Imposing order on White House operations, over-

Ed Meese and Leon Panetta

seeing the President's schedule, keeping track of the flow of people and paper to and from the Oval Office, negotiating on behalf of the President, and "taking the heat" for the President require a special type of individual.

Some chiefs of staff are remembered for the spectacular part they played in helping the President succeed in office. Others are known primarily for the unceremonious nature of their falls from grace. Surprisingly, Presidents often spend less time thinking about their choices for principal aides than they do for less important appointees they will seldom see after their confirmations. For reasons easily understandable, the chief of staff position and the people who have held it are attracting the attention of presidential scholars and journalists.

Leon Panetta sums up the role he played as Clinton's Chief of Staff in this way:

> The chief of staff performs functions crucial to the
> President: integrating policy and information; orga-
> nizing the White House; doling out office space,
> which of course is very contentious; guarding access
> to the President; making sure that there is no
> freelancing on the part of the White House staff. He
> is the presidential enforcer; takes heat for the Presi-
> dent—as former Carter Chief of Staff Jack Watson
> said, he is the President's javelin catcher—and has
> the stature to settle disputes among Cabinet secre-
> taries, which nobody else except for the President
> really can do.

James Pfiffner and most other analysts of the presidency argue that a chief of staff is essential today because the White House is such a large and complex organization, although it means that the President must give up some control. But Pfiffner adds a warning:

If a chief of staff takes a domineering approach to the office, there's going to be disaster. In my judgment, we've had four domineering chiefs of staff: Sherman Adams for Ike; H. R. Haldeman for Nixon; Don Regan for Reagan; and John Sununu for George Bush. Each of these chiefs of staff alienated the press. They alienated members of Congress. They often denigrated members of their own administration. Some of them had a reputation for a lack of civility. And each of them resigned in disgrace after doing serious harm to their Presidents.

So, the chief of staff is necessary, but that person, I would argue, should play a facilitating or a neutral broker type of role. [Examples include] Donald Rumsfeld, Dick Cheney, Jack Watson, James Baker, Mac McLarty, Leon Panetta, Erskine Bowles. The domineering approach is likely to lead to disaster.

The functions of a chief of staff, however, can take different forms. In the first Reagan term, key responsibilities were divided among three individuals. Ed Meese, as a member of this "troika," understood Reagan's logic:

The President came into office with some very clear objectives. He looked, at the outset, for a 180-day period, which happened to be the time between taking office on the 20th of January and the time that Congress normally leaves for recess in August. It was about a six-month period and he knew that in order to get his objectives accomplished, he had to get most of his program through in that period of time.

His objectives were basically threefold: to revitalize the economy; to rebuild our military capability; and to restore the United States' position of leadership in the world, particularly as it related to the Cold War. He organized his White House staff primarily based upon his experiences as governor, using a relatively structured system very similar to what President Eisenhower used.

Reagan's White House was shaped to carry out these specific objectives. And the work of developing the White House and its basic structure, as well as principles of operation, began during the transition. Among the first appointments he made, even before some of the Cabinet members, were the top three people in the White House staff.

We had what was called in the first term "the Troika," a name that was coined by the news media, but there were three of us who had the division of responsibilities on the top level of the White House staff. Mike Deaver had the responsibility for those things relating particularly to the President personally, things like scheduling and travel. Jim Baker, as Chief of Staff, had the responsibility for the administration of the White House and for the legislative, the press, and the communications responsibilities. I had the responsibility as counsellor to the President for policy development, the administration of the Cabinet, and the liaison with the executive branch.

Clinton chose the more traditional approach in designing the position. Under Panetta, the chief of staff had two deputies:

I established two deputy chiefs of staff. One was involved in political and in policy areas; that was Harold Ickes. The other was assigned to oversee largely the personnel operation in the White House, but also the scheduling operation, which is really significant in terms of setting the agenda for the President; that was Erskine Bowles and later Evelyn Lieberman.

The Chief of Staff's Daily Functions

Panetta says that the meetings and day-to-day functioning of the chief of staff, his deputies, and other senior staff is critical to the success of the White House:

There was a group of 14 or 15 key staff people that I met with at 7:30 each morning. Obviously, that included the chief of staff, myself. The chief of staff's responsibilities are those of not only overseeing the staff, the schedule, and operations of the White House, but also coordinating policy development.

Coordinating Policy Development. Panetta also explains the importance of carefully structured daily staff meetings to keep everyone focused in order to advance the President's strategy:

The primary purpose of that 7:30 a.m. meeting was to focus on a schedule, a summary of the schedule of events for the President that day; to discuss foreign policy issues that were taking place; to discuss economic issues; to discuss what was happening in the Congress; to discuss any legal issues that were coming up; and in addition to that, to focus on the event of the day for the presidency. In other words, the message of the day that the President wanted to get out in that particular event.

There was a second group of staff that we met with at 8:15. And the purpose of meeting with that second group was to ensure that they, too, were aware of the President's schedule and the events in each of the areas I discussed. They would report from their particular areas. That meeting included the following: the staff secretary, responsible for all of the documentation that flows through the White House; the Cabinet secretary, responsible for liaison to all of the Cabinet members; public liaison, an increasing role these days as the individual who is responsible for ensuring that every public interest group and every private key constituency is made aware of whatever decisions or events that are going to take place in the White House; intergovernmental liaison, which relates to the governors and all of the state and local officials; personnel and the various appointments that have to be made by the President; White House operations, the overall view of White House operations throughout the West Wing and the White House generally; the schedule and advance teams, another growing area because not only do you have to lay out the full schedule for the President, but you have to "advance" wherever that President goes; the Council on Environmental Quality; the National Science Advisor; the Office of National Drug Control Policy; the Military Office; what we call Walkout, which is a basic communications setup for the President wherever he goes; a social secretary; and then other supporting staff and aides.

Such routine meetings are well understood to be critically important, according to Panetta:

There was a reason why Bob Rubin, who used to attend these meetings in the morning as head of the NEC, asked that he could continue to attend the 7:30 meetings in the White House when he became Secretary of the Treasury. He understood that that was where a lot of the key decisions would be made, and he wanted to be a part of it. I think you're going to see proximity increase as a base of power. As a result, I think we have to recognize the reality that in the modern presidency, an effective and capable staff is going to be essential to an effective and capable presidency.

Imposing Order and Discipline. One of the most important daily functions of the chief of staff is imposing order and discipline in a situation prone to chaos. Panetta sees two possible approaches—but suggests that one is clearly superior to the other:

One is an informal approach in which there is open door approach to the staff, allowing them to have free access to the President, free access to briefings and discussions that take place with the President. This is a center-of-the-wheel kind of approach that

President Kennedy put in place, where he was at the center and allowed for access from a number of key assistants.

The other approach is a structured approach. The informal way has been compared to a soccer game in grammar school, where all of the kids go after the ball at the same time. And it can be very much that way if you try to provide a very informal approach in which everyone would have easy access to the President. It has to be structured and you have to have a disciplined approach to the responsibilities that are part and parcel of the staff.

The chief of staff's job in that light is not so much a management job as a battlefield position. The reality is that you have to have a sense of mission, of duty, of discipline. The staff has to remain focused, even though there may be incoming fire and a lot of issues that are breaking that are not necessarily related to what you want to have as the President's primary message for that day. Nevertheless, the staff has to be focused. They have to be disciplined and they have to continue to do their jobs. It is important, therefore, to establish a very clear chain of command and an organization chart in which each staff member knows who they are reporting to, who their supervisor is.

Among other tasks, then, Panetta saw himself as the chief enforcer of order and discipline:

[It's] important to establish rules regarding discipline, behavior, and access to the President, to briefings, to events, to Air Force One. There is always a natural tendency [to want to be] close to the President of the United States—you draw your energy source from being able to meet with the President of the United States. And the consequence is that any briefing with the President could result in as many as 25 or 50 people participating because that's the place to be. But you have to limit that tendency.

You can't get the business of the White House done unless those who participate in the briefings are only those who, in fact, have a responsibility for that particular issue. The same thing is true of travelling in Air Force One. People want to be able to be on the plane, to be able to have that opportunity. It's understandable but, at the same time, it can also result in chaos if you don't have only those who have a responsibility for that particular trip.

So you have to establish clear lines of discipline and behavior for access to the President. You have to assure that the briefings for the President are well-prepared, well-organized, brief, clear, direct, and that they present a set of options to the President so that he can ultimately make the decision. He's got to face a number of key decisions throughout the day. In order for that to happen in a smooth and effective way, briefings have to be well structured. When I was chief of staff, my approach was to have the briefing presented to me in the chief of staff's office, so that I could then see what kind of presentation would be made, what the options were and try to tighten it up as much as possible for presentation to the President.

Part of imposing order and discipline, adds Panetta, is making sure that the President's schedule allows him to stay focused over time:

The bully pulpit works, but it only works if it's focused and if it has a clear message and a clear event and a clear direction for the President that day. If he does too much, the message is not clear. If he focuses on one or two key events, then the message is clear to the public and to the country.

For that reason, it is important to establish discipline with regard to the schedule. And that means that you have to focus not only on today's schedule, tomorrow's schedule, next week's schedule, but the schedule of the President for the next four to six months. What are the invitations, the key events, the key activities that are going to involve the President of the United States? In fact, we even looked at the schedule for six to twelve months, to really begin to establish what activities the President would be focusing on over that period of time.

On the other hand, senior staff can easily end up organizing the President's time, access, and options so that their influence can be excessive. The new President should be wary of this. Michael Barone has a tongue-in-cheek solution:

I would like to add as my one small contribution to the political science of the presidency the rule (I would call it the Barone Rule, naturally) that every set of options must contain an even number of choices. I think there is a certain Goldilocks tendency to this: One is too hot, one is too cold, and one is just right. That tends to lead to manipulation. For example, option A is to have all-out nuclear war with the Soviet Union and also send 5 million troops across the line. Option C is give away all of America's nuclear weapons to the Soviet Union and open our borders to the Red Army of China. And then there's option B. And guess what? Option B tends to be the option that the apparatchik who put together the option list has had as his pet project since he was an assistant professor at Squino College. If you give people an even number of options, they've got to do something that's at least a little asymmetric.

Moreover, a large and powerful staff within the White House is a mixed blessing for a President. Any new occupant of the White House should ponder the observations of James Pfiffner:

I see four central paradoxes of the modern presidency. [First,] with respect to the White House, the biggest threats to a President and an administration's legacy do not come from external enemies. They come from inside the White House: often overzealous loyalists, in the case of Watergate and Iran–Contra, or the President himself, in the case the Lewinsky affair.

[Second], with respect to the Cabinet, the best way to control the executive branch is to delegate as many issues as possible to Cabinet secretaries and keep in close touch with them. The White House should be selective and reserve presidential intervention for high priority issues. If the White House tries to control everything, it will get overwhelmed.

Third, with respect to political appointments, the President has to set the tone for the types of people that should be selected, but he ought to delegate, in my judgment, much of the subcabinet recruitment to Cabinet secretaries. The competence of administration officials will do much more for the President's reputation and legacy than will superficial loyalty. And fourth, with respect to the career services, a new administration should not see career civil servants as the enemy or obstacles to be overcome, but should expect their enthusiastic support. And the sooner political appointees reach a cooperative accommodation with them, the sooner the President's agenda can be enforced and accomplished.

PARTICIPANTS

Staffing a New Administration
May 16, 2000
St. Regis Hotel
Washington, D.C.

Presenters

VERONICA BIGGINS
*Former Director of Presidential Personnel for
President Bill Clinton*

E. PENDLETON JAMES
*Former Director of Presidential Personnel for
President Ronald Reagan*

THE HONORABLE EDWIN MEESE III
Former Counsellor, President Ronald Reagan

CHASE UNTERMEYER
*Former Director of Presidential Personnel for
President George Bush*

Commentators

JAMES KING
*Former Director of the Office of Personnel Management for
President Bill Clinton*

PAUL LIGHT
*Vice President and Government Studies Director,
The Brookings Institution*

JAMES P. PFIFFNER
*Professor of Government and Public Policy,
George Mason University*

CHAPTER III:
STAFFING A
NEW ADMINISTRATION

"Begin quickly. Get the infrastructure before the election, because the day after the election everything is going to hit the fan and resumes are going to start rolling in."
—James Pfiffner

Immediately after their election, Presidents-elect begin deciding whom they wish to serve in their administration. They find no shortage of people willing to provide suggestions: campaign workers and officials, political contributors, Members of Congress, governors, mayors, friends and relatives, friends of relatives, and relatives of friends. They also receive thousands of unsolicited resumes.

The days immediately following a presidential election are hardly the optimal time for a President-elect and his advisers to be making personnel decisions. They are usually exhausted at the end of a grueling campaign. But positions must be filled, and if these decisions are postponed or ignored, mistakes will be made. There will be delay and indecision, making possible future embarrassments and even scandal.

In the simpler past, political parties regarded most positions whose occupants served at the pleasure of the President as patronage and filled them in a manner reminiscent of Andrew Jackson's "spoils" system. At that time, however, the federal government was minimal both in size and in the impact it exerted over American life. As it took on more functions in the 20th century, its bureaucracy grew, as did the number of political appointees to oversee it.

Today, a President-elect appoints as many as 6,000 people to government positions, and about half of these are critical to the operations of the executive branch. Some speak of this proliferation as a product of "title creep." Yet others insist that in a republic, a leader can translate his mandate into policy only by having at his disposal sufficient followers in the executive branch to ensure that his will is carried out.

The increase in the number of presidential appointments, and the increased specialization required of incumbents, have led modern President to depart from earlier methods for filling jobs. Beginning with the Kennedy Administration, incoming Presidents began to regard "staffing up" as much a manner of recruitment as a reward for the faithful. The

From left to right: Al Felzenberg, Pendleton James, Paul Light, Ed Meese, James Pfiffner, Jim King, Chase Untermeyer, and Veronica Biggins

Kennedy Administration's modest operation—based on three "talent scouts"—was a precursor to the modern Office of Presidential Personnel. Begun under Richard Nixon, the office peaked at 100 employees in the beginning of Ronald Reagan's first term in office.

Presidents have given different directives to those assisting them in staffing an administration. Some let Cabinet officers pick their principal aides and staff their departments; often, they later complained that the political appointees owed their primary allegiance to people other than the President. Other Presidents chose to control all non-civil service hiring from the White House; they went to great lengths to ensure that their appointees functioned as a team.

Some Presidents, notably Ronald Reagan, gave instructions that political appointees should not only be competent, but that they should share the administration's ideological objectives. Others, like Bill Clinton, placed a premium on ethnic, gender, and, often, geographic diversity. Still others placed a heavy emphasis on personal associations, long-time service, and comfort level with the President.

Rarely does the announcement of a President's intent to appoint someone to a post mean that a position will be filled soon. There are forms to be completed, statutory ethical requirements to be met, background investigations, and Senate confirmation hearings and votes. Studies suggest that this process has led to increased delays and is more contentious. Moreover, appointees stay in their posts for shorter periods. Presidents today find the personnel function is more of an ongoing than a transitional enterprise. As a result, there have been calls for changes in the methods by which appointees are screened, cleared, and assessed. At least one presidential commission and several think tanks and foundations have put forward proposals to revise the system.

THE IMPORTANCE OF EARLY PLANNING

While Kennedy may have been more systematic than his predecessors in creating a team to select staff for his Administration, it was still a small operation. When Richard Nixon was elected, the process was what Pendleton James, who later served in the personnel office under Nixon, described as a BOGSAT system—a "Bunch of Guys Sitting Around the Table" after the election selecting staffers.

Pendleton James, Chase Untermeyer, and Veronica Biggins

In contrast, by April 1980—before Ronald Reagan even received the Republican presidential nomination—senior aide Edwin Meese had contacted Pendleton James, requesting that he put together a staffing plan for the Administration. It was so early in the election year that James did not think it was a serious request until a month or so later when Meese asked him for his report:

> So I was embarrassed. I thought, "My God, he's serious!" So I did a five-page report, and basically it analyzed the process of the transition, staffing the administration, but more than anything else it outlined what could be done between then, which was May 1980, and when Reagan took office.

> So what could be done then, and if he got the nomination what could be done between the nomination and the transition, and then the transition through the inaugural? That's basically what it outlined.

James took charge of Reagan's search for appointment candidates, and he became Director of Presidential Personnel. After

Reagan's nomination was assured, he started to put his plan into action. One of his first and most important actions was to supplement the list of people already known to Reagan and the campaign with a talent bank of experts. James explains his reasoning as follows:

> We needed to develop a nationwide talent bank. And when you look at that talent bank, the men and women that come into the administration, they're not all Washington lawyers; they're not all Washington lobbyists.

> There's a great need for substantive talent throughout the nation to serve in the Executive Office of the President. You need people who are experts in the field of agriculture, science, technology, nuclear, chemistry, trade; all facets of business and academic life are needed in certain segments of the administration. So we put together a rather large talent bank.

> Now, let me say we do not talk to people, we do not interview people, we do not ask for people to apply; but I'm a headhunter in real life, and I do this for a living. So we put together who are the leaders in the field of agriculture, who are the leaders in defense, foreign policy, economic trade, and things like that, and came together with a long list of names. There is no science to it but developing a bank that we could draw upon.

> None of these were political; none of them came out of the campaign. You get plenty of that feedback. You don't have to search for those. So if we did win the election, we would have that bank to go through.

James's team also focused on the positions that Reagan, if elected, would need to fill first in order to move forward quickly and decisively on issues at the top of his agenda. Economic policies were the top priority, says James, so he concentrated on the economic slots:

> What was the major policy issue facing Ronald Reagan in 1980? It was economic policy, if you all remember, and I'm sure you do. So we identified out of the 400 or 500 appointments what were the key 87 positions that impinged upon economic policy, be that in agriculture or defense, State, Treasury, or whatever. We wanted to make sure we got those appointments up first so that they got confirmed first so that they could be legally empowered to help on those policies.

Criteria for Selection

According to James, the Reagan team applied a set of five criteria—philosophical commitment, integrity, toughness, competence, and being a team player—to the initial list of candidates to determine who would be included in the short list for administration positions:

> Number one, philosophical commitment to Ronald Reagan. In other words, if you're coming in to serve in this Administration, you know what Reagan ran on. You know what his campaign policies are; you know what his speeches were; you know what he wants to accomplish, because all political candidates outline that during the political campaign. Are you philosophically compatible with this program that this President has outlined? That was one criterion.

> Second, we would appoint men and women of unquestioned integrity from the moral background and capability and lifestyle to be sure that they had integrity.

> The third criterion was toughness. By toughness we meant the ability to withstand the buffeting you take in the executive branch. Men and women who serve in these high-level posts are buffeted daily by special-interest groups, by Congressmen, by some committee chairman, by lawyers who want to influence your policy for their direction or for their clients. So by toughness we meant the ability to hang in there, withstand that buffeting as much as you can, to adhere to the President's program.

> The fourth criterion was competence. Obviously you had to have something in your background, training, and experience that gave you the ability to understand the substantive nature of that particular post you would have to take.

> And the fifth criterion was being a team player. By "team player" we meant you're not taking this appointment for your own self-aggrandizement, which is a byproduct of any senior-level post anyhow, but you recognize that you're there to work with a team, to work with a commitment, and try to accomplish what the President's agenda is. You're not off the reservation enhancing your own political career or seeking that job you're looking for after you leave the administration.

Selecting Cabinet Officers

The Reagan team put the selection of Cabinet officials on a separate track, outside the normal transition operation. James began by identifying the pool of nationally known individuals who were capable of running Cabinet departments, who were well-known to Reagan, and who were philosophically committed to Reagan:

> I put together—hypothetically, again—without talking to people, without interviewing people, three to seven names for each department: State, Defense, Treasury. Many times there are duplicates. For example, obviously you knew Cap [Caspar] Weinberger was going to be on that list. Well, I had Cap under State, Defense, and OMB. You could put him in either one, or Bill Casey, or whatever it may be.

> The day after the election, we were all out in California at the Century Plaza Hotel. The next morning, a meeting took place at the President-elect's residence in Pacific Palisades. Subject: Cabinet selection. At that meeting in his living room were Mike Deaver, Jim Baker, George Bush, Paul Laxalt, Bill Casey, and myself and the President-elect, and I had the report.

> Everybody in that room had been focusing all their time on getting the man elected. They were not thinking about anything else except votes, fund-raising, ballots, electoral college. Now, all of a sudden, "Gee, now we've got to put together a team." So by doing just the staff work, now we had the names. We passed it around, and then for the first time the President-elect started focusing on Cap here or Bill Casey there, or Al Haig or Don Regan here, or Drew Lewis, and the process went on.

Preparing for the Press

It is very important, says Chase Untermeyer, who headed the Office of Presidential Personnel under President Bush, to remember that personnel is always a news story. He suggests that the President select someone to handle the media:

> It also seems to me inevitable that Presidential Personnel will be a big news story during the transition and the immediate post-inaugural period, deep into the first year of the administration. It is also inevitably a bad story, particularly as in recent administrations where it's taken ever longer to fill positions.

> It seems to me, therefore, that one essential element of a Presidential Personnel Office would be a full-time press person to field the calls that will come in with what I used to call the body counts: "How many vacancies are still open? How many women have you selected? How many minorities are selected? How many people from Ohio have been selected?" These can occupy the day of the Director

of Presidential Personnel, who has a few other things to do, such as interviewing people, attending meetings, taking calls from Senators, and all the rest.

I came to the conclusion that I could do one of two things. I could be the Director of Presidential Personnel or I could take care of my press relations, but I could not do both. And my press relations suffered, which was the right choice, but it seems to me that because the President's own standing and image of the administration is so key, that is extremely vital.

PRESIDENTIAL CONTROL OF STAFF SELECTIONS

The President has the authority to select whomever he wishes for staff positions that do not require Senate confirmation, and it is he who formally nominates officials who must be confirmed. In reality, of course, the President faces practical political constraints in his choices. In addition to considerations triggered by public and congressional perceptions, a new President also encounters pressure from two key groups, his own Cabinet and his campaign organizations, for non-Cabinet positions. How the President responds to this pressure can have a lasting impact on his administration.

Pressure from the Cabinet

The pressure from Cabinet secretaries to control their own staff appointments can be intense, says George Mason University professor of government James Pfiffner. In part this is a simple "turf battle." Yet if a Cabinet secretary is to be held accountable for his agency, then, some argue, the secretary should be able to assemble his own management team. Pfiffner explains the Cabinet secretary's viewpoint, as described by Frank Carlucci, who served as Secretary of Defense late in the Reagan Administration:

> The Cabinet secretary position has been articulated by Frank Carlucci in a National Academy of Public Administration interview in the 1980s. We were asking him his advice for new political appointees coming into an administration, and he said, "Spend most of your time at the outset focusing on the personnel system, get your appointees in place, have your own political personnel person, because the first clash you're going to have is with the White House Personnel Office; and I don't care whether you're a Republican or a Democrat, if you don't get your own people in place you're going to end up being a one armed paper-hanger."

Some President have shared this view and allowed Cabinet secretaries to appoint their department positions. One such President was Jimmy Carter. But Carter's Director of White House Personnel, James King, explains that the Carter Administration learned a hard lesson from that approach:

> President Carter believed that the Cabinet [secretaries] should appoint their own folks, and that made it much easier in personnel. What you got, basically, was to carry a mop and a broom and clean up after everyone. Obviously, you learn from that experience, and I'm very grateful you did. The citizens of this country are better served.
>
> One of the great myths is, "The buck will stop here if I've got my own team out there," and that's the argument from the Cabinet. The buck doesn't stop there. The buck stops with the President, plain and simple, and you're putting the integrity of the administration, its future, and the trust of the American people on the line.

Building a loyal Cabinet is, of course, critical to a President's success. The Reagan Administration understood this well, and Reagan's top White House staff took steps to ensure that the Cabinet worked closely with the White House in carrying out the President's agenda (see Chapter 4). Reagan, however, believed that it was equally important that the first loyalty of a Cabinet secretary's staff should be to the President. Key agency staffers, then, should owe their jobs, as well as their loyalty, to the President rather than the Cabinet secretary. Pendleton James explains that the Reagan White House made sure they controlled the agency positions from the beginning of the process:

> How did we get control of the appointment process? This was key. The President decided, "I'll hypothetically pick Don Regan Secretary of the Treasury." Don came in, sat down with the President. Ed Meese and Pen James were in the room. And the President said, "Don, congratulations, I want you to be my Secretary of Treasury. You're a great guy. We're going to have a great team, we're going to do this, we're going to do that."
>
> He said, "One thing I want you to understand, though." This is the President talking: "We are going to control the appointments here at the White House, and Pen is going to be head of Presidential Personnel. Now, Don, we want your input on who you want for your Deputy, Assistant Secretary, and such, because it's your team and you have a part, but we are going to control it here at the Oval Office, and do you agree with us?" And, of course, every one of them says, "Yes, I really do."
>
> So we got control of it right away. Obviously, you lose that after about nine months or so, but for the

first six or eight months, that Cabinet officer is going to clear it with us before he does anything.

In order to appoint staff this way, however, the President must follow a systematic process and not allow himself to bypass the process, as, for instance, when lobbied by an old friend. After Reagan succumbed to such pleading once or twice, a more formal White House clearance procedure was put in place:

> All the names suggested, whether they came from the President himself or from the Cabinet officers, came into the process. The process was controlled by Baker, Deaver, Meese, and James. Every day ... at five o'clock weekdays, we met in Jim Baker's office. In that meeting, there were only the four of us. Nobody else was ever invited or attended that meeting. It was a closed-door session unless by special request that we bring somebody in who had a particular point to make and he was invited by Ed or Mike or Jim.

> At that time, books would have been prepared by my staff over in the OEB [Old Executive Office Building] saying, "Today we are looking at the Assistant Secretary for whatever." First page in the book was what is the job, what is the job description, what is his authority? The second page was the candidate, his or her background, capabilities, whatever. The third page was political support, who's been lobbying to get this appointment, who was for him, who was against him. And the fourth page, what they always looked at first, was who else was considered, because instead of coming in with just one name, other people were considered in the pipeline.

> It would be at that five o'clock staff meeting that the President's senior team would make a judgment as to whom they would recommend to the President. Every Tuesday and Thursday, I met with the President, and at that time we went through the process. Sometimes Ed or Mike or Jim would be in there, or me, or by ourselves. Then he would approve or ask for more options. So that was the other process on controlling.

Untermeyer agrees that Cabinet secretaries and the White House can easily come into conflict, and that the personnel staff must be ready and equipped to deal with this:

> As a practical matter, Cabinet officers are very politically sophisticated and often have held important positions as governors or panjandrums on Capitol Hill. They have coteries and teams of their own, who

they very much want to see with them in those departments and agencies.

At the same time, the Presidential Personnel Office is hoping to take care of those brave volunteering souls who slept on floors in New Hampshire and who expect to be and would love to be Assistant Secretary for Press or Congressional Liaison and who then come smash up against the Cabinet Secretary, who has other names in mind, maybe somebody who's even against the winning candidate and may well have been tittering about the candidate's foibles in some cocktail party here in Washington.

This is the inevitable clash against which the Director of Presidential Personnel must be armed with the lists. If not, if the Cabinet officer selectees arrive in that initial meeting with the lists of their team from Capitol Hill or Wall Street or wherever else they may have been, it may be extremely difficult then to fight the battle you need to fight for your own folks.

Pressure from the Campaign

In addition to pressure from his Cabinet, the President will face pressure from his campaign staff to make certain appointments. This pressure will come not only from key campaign aides, but from the hundreds or thousands of people who worked hard at some level in the campaign. As James Pfiffner warns:

The most ferocious pressure, finally, comes from the campaign. This is legitimate pressure, because these people have worked to get the President elected, and they feel that they have a legitimate claim—and they certainly have a legitimate claim—to be considered. But the reality is that you can never do enough for campaigners. There are too many of them, and there's always going to be lingering resentments from those who think that they were owed an appointment.

Pfiffner adds that it is important to understand the different requirements of campaigns and government:

I agree with the idea of the politics of running as opposed to the politics of governing, and that governance is very different. If you get driven by the campaign side, you can end up with people who are very gifted working the system in a questionable fashion.

James King, the Director of Presidential Personnel for Jimmy Carter, explains some of the many reasons that an administration should be hesitant about hiring campaign workers:

The problem is, in a campaign, the kinds of people that can drop their family or maybe they haven't started a family, drop their job—maybe they don't have a full career going—and work full-time on the campaign. Those people are great to have, but they may not have the level of maturity or experience in the private sector, local, state government, and so forth that you want at the top level. So the key, I think, is to act as a casting director and choose who is right at which slots and what levels in terms of the talent.

Chase Untermeyer, however, feels that it is important to select people who have been close to the candidate, philosophically and on the campaign trail. (Chapter 1 discusses this issue in the context of the transition.) Still, he notes that this can ruffle feathers during a "friendly takeover," when the White House stays under the control of the same party. While he discounts stories that the Bush teams systematically fired people who had worked for Reagan, he points out that an incoming President will want his own people:

> I think this is the inevitable consequence of a friendly transition but I do believe that it is inevitable that a new President is going to come into office, even if that new President is the Vice President, with people who have been on the campaign circuit, who have been out there campaigning in the snows of New Hampshire and the cornfields of Iowa, wherever it may be, and who expect to be and will be rewarded.

> Meanwhile, there are loyal supporters of the incumbent President who have been toiling away honorably and faithfully at their desks here in Washington who, for whatever reason, did not want to resign and go off to Iowa and New Hampshire and nevertheless do their jobs. Those are the people who may feel abused when the new team comes in.

Inflated expectations from campaign staff can become a sudden and intense problem for the new White House team, and particularly for the Office of Presidential Personnel. Pendleton James recalls the acrimony he faced:

> During the transition of Reagan the regional political directors, referred to as RPDs, were very unhappy with Pen James. Number one, they didn't know who I was and why I had that job, because I wasn't visible in the campaign and appeared after the election; and, second, they weren't getting appointments, and all these other people, some of them holdovers and some of them from the Nixon years, were getting

these appointments, and they were very angry and very vocal.

I knew I had to face this. So I said the only way I can do it is call them all into a room—and there was a group bigger than this number here—and let me talk to them, because they have to understand: Yes, they have worked in the campaign; yes, they've slept on the floors; yes, they've carried the banners; yes, they've done the field work; but in the appointment process, in the beginning, we had to get the Cabinet first, and then we had to get the sub-Cabinet because most of these would be at an assistant secretary level or below, generally speaking.

It is important for the President's team to explain to campaign staffers why they should not see themselves as a conquering army, taking jobs as plunder. James recalls his efforts to convey this kind of message:

I said, "You've got to be patient because until we get these strata done, we can't get around to your appointments, because you will be appointed Schedule C's [non-career positions] and SES's [Senior Executive Service]." I had Senator Paul Laxalt go with me, because I didn't dare go by myself because I wasn't a member of that group. And Paul talked to them.

There was one guy on the front row who I didn't know, who stood up, turned around to his colleagues and former RPDs. They were angry. These guys were physically angry. And he said, "All right, knock it off. I understand what Pen is saying. There has to be an order. There has to be a process. We're going to get our turn. Now, be quiet and be patient."

With that, Paul and I were walking out of the room, and I turned to Paul and I said, "Who was that guy? I could have kissed him." He said that was Lee Atwater. Lee Atwater was an RPD at that time, not the world-famous guy we know today, but he was the only one that really understood there had to be an order in the process: Yes, the campaign workers are going to get a job, but they are not going to get on board in the first 100 days of the administration.

James Pfiffner adds that the experiences of recent administrations and the scope of the staffing challenge facing a new President suggest four guidelines for a new administration:

First begin quickly. Get the infrastructure before the election, because the day after the election everything is going to hit the fan and resumes are going to start rolling in.

Second, expect the Cabinet Secretaries are going to be assertive about their appointments, but have the President lay down the ground rules early so that they understand that the final decision is in the Office of Presidential Personnel and, of course, the President.

Third, expect pressure from the campaign and from the Hill and be ready to get back to important recommenders to explain exactly why Senator X's favorite nephew cannot be appointed to be Assistant Secretary of Y Department.

Finally, the role of the President is crucial. He or she has to set the tone for appointments and intervene when it's important ... but you let the Office of Presidential Personnel act as a buffer to deflect patronage pressures away from him. That is, let the President make the decisions and OPP take the heat.

THE CONFIRMATION PROCEDURE

The incoming administration has an enormous number of positions to fill. As Pfiffner explains:

Each President has about 5,000 or 6,000 political appointments that he or she can make. Many of these, of course, are part-time and not all presidential appointments with consent of the Senate. They don't all go through OPP, the Office of Presidential Personnel. But about 3,000 people are crucial to running the executive branch: about 1,000 PAs [Presidential Appointees], about 1,400 Schedule C's, about 700 non-career Senior Executive Service. And, of course, the job of the Office of Presidential Personnel has increased greatly since 1981 when Pendleton James and Ronald Reagan decided that they were going to control everything, including the non-presidential appointments; that is, non-career SES and Schedule C positions.

As a result, there is enormous pressure to move quickly so that the new President can put his stamp on the government early in his administration and not lose valuable time or momentum. The urgency is more acute, adds Pfiffner, because the length and complexity of the confirmation process have increased considerably:

There's a great need to get your people on board soon. The leadership of the executive branch has to be there if you want to be in control of it, and the data show that the time between a presidential nomination and Senate confirmation has been increasing. Cal McKenzie's data show Kennedy had about two and a half months average, and Bill Clinton about eight and a half months average. So it takes a long time, but nevertheless it's crucial to get those people out there because the civil servants are competent, they're capable, but they will not take the lead. That's not their role.

The process of filling these positions, says Brookings Institution Senior Fellow Paul Light, is now so slow and cumbersome that it has reached its breaking point and needs to be reformed:

Anybody who's familiar with this process would take 1984 in a heartbeat. The process then was a paragon of efficiency and distinctive attention to the quality of appointees. Today's process, I would argue, is designed to fail. It does not work. It has collapsed nearly completely. There are too many jobs, too many detours, too many forms, and too little institutional capacity, and I'd say to my colleagues from the White House that the White House does not control the Cabinet.

One of the consequences of the current system, says Light, is that Cabinet secretaries have sought to circumvent the deficiencies of the confirmation process by creating a shadow staff at the top level:

Cabinet officers invented a whole new class of title called the chief of staff. Now we have a double Cabinet. We have the Cabinet officers, who are selected through the White House process and subject to Senate advice and consent, who are appointing chiefs of staff and deputy chiefs of staff and assistant deputy chiefs of staff on down the line so that we have both the formal Cabinet that's subject to advice and consent and the informal Cabinet that now has sucked away many of the responsibilities that used to go to advice-and-consent appointees. The Senate should deal with it, and they should deal with it in part by accelerating their review process and also inspecting the overall number of appointees.

Many who have experienced or studied the appointment process agree that the time has come to review which positions need Senate confirmation. As top Reagan aide Edwin Meese says:

One suggestion has been the idea of looking at the number of top positions and looking at the whole structure of government and seeing if this can't be simplified and if there can't be a more rational basis for deciding which appointee should be subject to Senate confirmation and which should not be, and also to look at the superstructure of government that's grown up, including the people who have been a parallel organization to the presidential appointment and Senate confirmation system—the

chiefs of staff, the assistant chiefs of staff, deputy
chiefs of staff, and all the others that have grown
up—to see both what influence this has and how
this relates to a President and [the Office of] Presidential Personnel having control of the human
resources function and process throughout the government.

Avoiding Self-Inflicted Wounds

While congressional committees impose various and conflicting
requirements that slow down the process and create frustration,
says Chase Untermeyer, it is nevertheless important that the
incoming administration avoid adding to these problems. (See
Chapter 1.) For instance, the administration should move early to
make its own selections and get executive branch clearance:

There are definitely problems on the Senate side of
this, but the greater load of problems is all on the
executive branch side of things. I do believe that the
next administration should take the steps, many of
which have already been proposed ... to shorten the
process on the executive branch side in the selection
and clearance phase so that it can get names to the
Senate in a timely fashion, robbing the Senate at the
very least of the excuse of saying, "Why are you
blaming us for the delay in getting this person confirmed when the nomination didn't even come to
our desks until April 27th or some other late date?"

So that is the challenge for the next administration:
to make sure that it tightens up its system first
before confronting the Senate, at which time I
would like them to think that if there is a stack of
nominations pending on desks in the Senate, perhaps the Senate leadership would realize that they
then need to tighten up their own process and move
things faster, in which case we have a hope of
reversing the almost geometric increase in time it's
taken since the Kennedy Administration to get people through the process.

In addition, the appointment process can slow down if an
incoming President has made the makeup of his administration
an issue during his campaign, or if he makes a commitment during the transition. As Clinton's Assistant to the President and
Director of Presidential Personnel Veronica Biggins explains,
Clinton's campaign and transition promises were a factor in the
pace of selections in his Administration:

One of the things that Clinton said when he was first
inaugurated was that diversity, an administration
that "looked like America," was very important. We
spent a lot of time on the issue of diversity and

thinking very carefully and really sourcing, so some things took a little longer. But I do think that there were a lot of people that moved into the administration and developed, brought in skills, and brought a breadth of experience and diversity in this process that had not existed before and that really helped move this process along.

A new administration, says Untermeyer, can also ease the burden of the personnel process by taking a stand against the proliferation of positions—which itself spawns a flood of applications for jobs that can overwhelm a personnel office. He suggests a bold step:

I would recommend the next administration do what could be called zero-based personnel work in which all of the jobs that will be reported in the Plum Book, which is a snapshot of appointments held as of June 30, be erased so that the next administration coming into power will not have people applying for these titles but will begin with the basic sinews of the administration created by Congress— that is, the deputy and under- and assistant secretary positions, perhaps with a direction that you may not have any more than X-number of personal staff. Otherwise, there are going to be people who will be beating on the door, sending in their resumes to fill these positions which they will presume as a given in the federal structure.

In order to speed up the process, Untermeyer suggests, the next administration should make greater use of standardized forms and the Internet. Biggins very much agrees:

I recently had the opportunity to fill this form out, sitting there trying to find a friend to loan a typewriter to me or to figure out how to handwrite this whole process, and I had people say to me, "Why in the world?" So I go back to Chase Untermeyer's point in particular: Internet, Internet, Internet. Certainly there is a way that the White House and the Hill can come to an agreement on a mutual form that can be used, that is used across the board so that people aren't then filling out different forms for either side.

HELPING NOMINEES SURVIVE THE PROCESS

Finally, say those who have gone through or been involved in the confirmation process, it is important that the White House not think its job is over once names are formally submitted to the Senate for confirmation. Instead, the administration should both maintain a team dedicated to shepherding the nominations through Congress, and, equally important, keep up the spirits of the nominees during the lengthy, frustrating, and often demoralizing process. The team should help nominees understand the process on Capitol Hill and hold their hands throughout the confirmation process. As top Reagan aide Ed Meese emphasizes, nominees need plenty of guidance and support:

> Perhaps the most important aspect that came out of today's discussion was the importance not just, from the President's standpoint, of how you select [appointees], but also how you handle the nominee himself or herself—in other words the "care and feeding" of candidates, the survivor's guide ... laying out for the candidate what they are going to have to face before they get too far into it. But also [understanding] that on a continuing basis they have someone to hold their hand, a point of contact that they can turn to wherever they might be; the fact that they need a shepherd to guide them through the entanglements of government until they get finally to their destination, which is that seat in the office that they've been longing for, or at least where the President is willing to put them. And [also, the need] for them to understand that when they are around newspaper reporters, what they say may be translated in ways that might not be favorable.

PARTICIPANTS

Developing Domestic Policy Within an Administration
December 9, 1999
St. Regis Hotel
Washington, D.C.

THE HONORABLE EDWIN MEESE III
Former Counsellor, President Ronald Reagan

Presenter

MARTIN ANDERSON
Former Assistant to President Ronald Reagan for Policy Development

Commentators

COLIN CAMPBELL
Professor of Public Policy, Georgetown University

BOB FRANKEN
Congressional Correspondent, CNN

C. BOYDEN GRAY
Former Counsel to President George Bush

PAUL LIGHT
Vice President and Government Studies Director, The Brookings Institution

SUSAN J. TOLCHIN
Professor of Public Policy, George Mason University

SHIRLEY ANNE WARSHAW
Professor of Political Science, Gettysburg College

Chapter IV:
Turning the President's Agenda into Administration Policy

"We didn't do much policy development, and the reason was because the policy was already developed. ... When we got elected in the fall of 1980, we knew what he wanted to do, and our job was to figure out how to do it and when to do it, how to implement it, how to make happen what he wanted done."
—Martin Anderson

Presidents who have entered office with ambitious agendas often devised many of their policies over the course of their campaigns. Once elected, these types of Presidents find they must set a tone and an agenda for their administration and make sure that the arms of their executive branch agencies work together to carry out that agenda. For the most part, then, this is a process not of policy development but of policy implementation.

Perhaps the most profound transformations that the Great Depression, World War II, and the Cold War brought to the presidency was the increasing centralization of executive branch policy development within the White House. The increased participation of the White House staff in this area, however, brings the potential for conflict between a President and his Cabinet. Although many come into office promising a Cabinet government, every President has found that the classical version of Cabinet government is unworkable.

Yet by statute the Cabinet departments retain certain prescribed duties for which Congress and the public hold them accountable. This dichotomy between theory and practice explains why many Presidents and their advisers frequently voice frustration with their Cabinet officers. The administration expects the Cabinet officers to do the President's bidding but instead sees them as advocates for constituency groups and bureaucracies whose concerns do not parallel those of the administration. At the same time, Cabinet officers, who often are distinguished in their own right, resent that younger, often abrupt, and always unelected and "unconfirmed" White House aides could tell them what to do.

Given this tension, Presidents vary considerably in both the means they employ and the success they have in keeping their administrations functioning as a team. By all accounts, the Reagan Administration was more successful than most in having both its political appointees and the civil service carry out its directives.

DEVELOPING POLICY FOR THE PRESIDENT

The history of the presidency shows that the most successful Presidents made clear the direction they intended their administrations to follow prior to their election. Those who campaigned

Edwin Meese III

Martin Anderson

with a mixed or muddled message, or who ran with broad, general themes, had difficulty finding their stride once in office. In his memoirs, Samuel I. Rosenman, one of Franklin Roosevelt's principal advisers, traced the origins of at least a dozen New Deal programs to speeches FDR delivered in his first presidential campaign. The policy initiatives of other activist Presidents, such as Woodrow Wilson and Lyndon Johnson, unfolded similarly. Ronald Reagan elucidated the policies his Administration would pursue not only as a candidate, but also in the nearly twenty years he spent in public life.

As Martin Anderson, Reagan's domestic and economic adviser, explains, the Reagan Administration's policy team was in the business of policy implementation, not policy development:

> We didn't do much policy development, and the reason was because the policy was already developed. During the full five years of Reagan's campaign for the presidency and the 10 or 15 years before he became President, Ronald Reagan had been thinking about and talking about exactly what

he would do if he ever became President. When we got elected in the fall of 1980, we knew what he wanted to do, and our job was to figure out how to do it and when to do it, how to implement it, how to make happen what he wanted done.

Later on, as the new challenges and problems arose, the task turned to developing ways to cope with them, but not in the beginning.

As George Mason University Professor of Public Policy Susan Tolchin notes, the well-prepared agenda that Reagan brought to the White House made it significantly different from the Carter Administration as well as the Clinton Administration:

Reagan hit the ground running. He had a few policies. He had them developed by think tanks such as [The Heritage Foundation]. He knew what he wanted to do, and it was very efficient, and it wasn't confusing to the public.

I think Carter would change his mind between breakfast and lunch, lunch to dinner. It wasn't that he wasn't very smart. It is just that he was thinking all the time, and he might have genuinely changed his mind, which is fine; it's what I do when I write books. But this is such a large and unwieldy and confusing country that it is much better politically for a President to have a simple message, to do it, than for a President to do seat-of-the-pants policy development, which we have seen really with Carter and Clinton versus Reagan.

If the role of the policy staff is to work out the details of a President's agenda, rather than to create an agenda, then these advisers need to determine how best to lay out implementation choices for the President. From his experience with the Reagan White House, Anderson offers practical advice on making the best decisions:

The key to effective policymaking in the White House [involves] two things. One is the information you have, and two is the access to the President. The President makes all the major decisions, and those decisions are made on the basis of what he knows and the information he receives.

To make a compelling case, a policy adviser has to have good, timely information. It must be relevant to the issue at hand. It must be comprehensive, and it must be accurate. And it should be presented in a balanced way, because it is important for a President to know what the downside is as well as the upside of all of the policies.

Policy information comes from a myriad of sources. It must be collected, judged, sorted, and reassembled to make a coherent, compelling case. But all of the best information in the world is worthless until and unless it is conveyed to the President. There are three basic ways to do this.

The best way is in person. The best and most effective way is to talk to him privately and directly. But that is an option that is available to only a very few people in the White House. During the Reagan years, one of those people was Ed Meese. There were a lot of times when he could just sit down with President Reagan and talk to him directly. But usually, those people are also extremely busy, and they don't have time to collect and process the extraordinary amount of policy information that has to be done.

The second way is by written memos. You can carefully write down everything and send it in. But the time a President has to read memos is limited, and the written word does have limitations. My own personal view is that written memos are usually not very effective.

That leaves the third one: meetings. I think the most practical way to convey information to a President is through meetings, through Cabinet meetings, through sub-Cabinet meetings, ad hoc staff meetings, meetings with outside advisory groups. A meeting attended by a President affords an excellent opportunity to present lots of information in a balanced way, subject to the cross-examination of all the other people that are in the meeting.

THE CABINET AS AN EFFECTIVE POLICYMAKING TOOL

The Cabinet can be a powerful instrument in enabling a President to implement an agenda—provided that its members are selected, organized, and utilized in the manner most conducive to unity and teamwork. Some Presidents voice frustration at their Cabinet officers' tendency to voice the concerns and protect the interests of their department's constituencies. To circumvent this obstacle, some Cabinet officers have disregarded, sometimes to their later regret, the statutory obligations they were required to fulfill.

Of the postwar Presidents, Eisenhower and Reagan had the greatest succees in having the Cabinet and the White House working in unison. For both Presidents, creative organization and careful use of staff members allowed them to synchronize the efforts of the Cabinet and the White House. Both spent a great deal of time in meetings with Cabinet members. Eisenhower met with his officers in Cabinet meetings, while Reagan met with Cabinet officers grouped in specially selected councils around a certain issue. Reagan and his advisers created these Cabinet Councils as vehicles through which policy could win acceptance and achieve implementation throughout the executive branch, according to Anderson:

> Most national policy issues cut across many, if not all, Cabinet departments, and a full Cabinet meeting is not appropriate. So what to do? In the Reagan Administration, on the foreign policy and defense side, the traditional National Security Council was used to organize and implement national security policy, and Richard Allen was the National Security Adviser. But on the economic and domestic side, a new strategy was developed to deal with the complexity of all of those domestic issues that face any President.

The Reagan Administration based this strategy on a refined version of the Cabinet Councils first introduced in the Nixon Administration. Anderson describes the structure under Reagan as follows:

> A Cabinet Council is really a smaller, tailor-made version of the Cabinet. Each council was designed to deal with specific issues of national policy. The Cabinet members, who comprised the councils, represented those departments that were most involved in the issue under discussion, but each Cabinet Council, like the Cabinet itself, was chaired by the President. In addition, each Cabinet Council also had a designated chair, another member of the Cabinet, who could act in the absence of the President.
>
> This gave these councils one special advantage over the Cabinet. A council could meet and discuss policy matters without the President being at the meeting. No decisions were made when the President was absent, but it was a powerful way to have preliminary discussion and distill the key issues to present to the President when he did attend.
>
> In fact, if you look back over the first couple of years, the President actually attended and chaired about one-fifth of all of those Cabinet Council meetings. Usually, they were meetings that were dealing with an especially important issue or meetings that had come to the point where a decision had to be made.

Anderson argues that the Cabinet Council system was central to making President Reagan's Cabinet operate effectively:

During the early years of the Reagan Administration, we had six of those Cabinet Councils: one on economic affairs, one on natural resources and the environment, one on commerce and trade, one on human resources, the fifth one on food and agriculture, and a final one on legal policy. All economic and domestic policy was funneled through those Cabinet Councils, and I think, the Cabinet Councils were a fairly elegant solution to the problem of how to effectively use Cabinet members in the development and implementation of the President's national policy goals.

Building a Loyal Cabinet Team

The Cabinet Council system also recognizes the importance of divorcing the President's top-level team members from their bureaucracies so that they can remain focused on the President's agenda.

As Gettysburg College Professor of Political Science Shirley Anne Warshaw explains:

> The problem is you have an enormous bureaucracy, 99 percent of which is civil service. It is very easy for Cabinet officers and sub-Cabinet officers, the deputy secretaries, the undersecretaries, the assistant secretaries, and those very few political appointees, to be co-opted by their own bureaucracy. They easily become attuned to the problems that their departments are concerned about.

> Although the President of the United States may say this budget deficit is a very serious problem, the issues in your department overwhelm you. When the President says to the Secretary of Agriculture, "I want to cut agricultural subsidies," but all of the farmers' groups and the Grange groups come to the Secretary of Agriculture and say, "We can't live without the subsidies," what does the Secretary of Agriculture do? Cabinet secretaries historically side with their departments, their clientele, the old iron triangle.

In a process that Nixon's top aide John Ehrlichman referred to as "marrying the natives," Cabinet officers often align with their departments rather the White House staff. As Warshaw says:

> The problem is, the President too often brings people from the campaign into the White House, often younger people. Then he brings in Cabinet officers who the White House staff don't know, and those Cabinet officers immediately ally with their departments rather than with the White House staff.

The Reagan White House team refined the Nixon system of Cabinet Councils. Under the Reagan system, Cabinet Councils were not just an efficient policymaking tool; they were also seen as a way of resisting the centrifugal forces on Cabinet officers—thereby galvanizing Cabinet support for the President's agenda. For example, they recognized how important it was that senior agency officials be physically present in the White House when critical decisions were made—and not in their own departments—so that they could pursue the President's agenda rather than their agency's.

As Martin Anderson explains, this necessitated that Cabinet Council meetings—not just full Cabinet meetings—be held at the White House to build a team around the President and his policies:

> We often heard that when you are talking about real estate, location is the key factor, and in meetings on national policy, the locations of the meetings can be a key factor. All meetings of the Cabinet Councils took place in the West Wing of the White House, usually in the Roosevelt Room, which is just outside the Oval Office, or in the Cabinet Room.

> In fact, during Reagan's first year in office, there were 112 Cabinet Council meetings, all held in the White House. The practical consequences of this were that on 112 occasions, a half a dozen or so Cabinet heads left their departments, climbed in the back seat of their chauffeured cars, and made their way over to the White House. This is an extraordinary number of times for a Cabinet head to come to the White House—far more than would have occurred if he or she were just going to Cabinet meetings or to other meetings called for a special purpose.

> The 10 and 15 minutes before the Cabinet Council meeting began, and the time after the Cabinet Council meeting had occurred, was a special time that Cabinet heads could interact closely with the senior White House staff to exchange views. They settled other business and generally got to know each other personally. In fact, sometimes I think that more business was done before the meeting and just after the meeting than during the meeting.

> This may seem like a small thing, but it can turn out—and I think it did—to be a crucial factor in providing and facilitating the policy process. These meetings provided an unusual degree of harmony between two normally antagonistic groups, the White House senior staff and the Cabinet. It also

enhanced the status and prestige of the Cabinet heads within their own departments.

Every time you had one of those 112 council meetings, the Cabinet head could say truthfully that he would personally go to the White House to meet with the President and the senior White House staff. It was an important symbolic act. All major policy discussions took place in the White House, far from the fiefdoms of the Cabinet. Every meeting re-emphasized that this was the President's business. It was his policy agenda.

Shirley Warshaw explains the effect that the top Reagan team desired with this Cabinet Council structure:

[They] wanted all of these Cabinet officers and these deputy secretaries to come into the White House, [and] if you were a reporter and said "Who are you?" to a Cabinet officer, they would say, "I am President Reagan's Secretary of Agriculture." It was important that the first thing they thought is that I am President Reagan's, and everything I do is President Reagan's. If you say I am simply the Secretary of Agriculture, it implies that your first loyalty is to the Department of Agriculture.

The Cabinet secretaries' attitudes were critical to the success of the Reagan Administration, says Warshaw:

[The Reagan team] didn't have that many major policies, but the list that they said they were going to do, they did. And they did that largely because of this issue of governance and the ability of Martin Anderson and the White House staff to bring those Cabinet officers on board. "This is what we are going to do, and you are behind me, right?" And they all said, "Absolutely."

That Cabinet Council structure was brilliant. It worked, and every single President since then has modeled after it.

THE VITAL ROLE OF PROPER STAFFING

Central to the success of the Reagan Cabinet Councils was the way they were staffed and organized. As Reagan's chief domestic policy assistant Martin Anderson explains:

The key to making the Cabinet Councils work was staffing. We had to figure out the best way to conduct and distribute the detailed policy studies and analyses that the Cabinet members would use to make intelligent recommendations to the President. Then you get to handle the logistic work necessary to keep the system running smoothly. We had to set the agenda for council meetings, set the times and the dates of those meetings, notify everyone in a timely fashion, take minutes of those meetings, and keep records.

The administrative support for the Cabinet Councils came out of Ed Meese's office. At the time, [National Security Adviser] Dick Allen on the foreign policy and defense side and myself on the economic and domestic policy side both reported directly to Ed, who then had the title of Counsel to the President.

On the domestic and economic policy side, the office which I headed, which was called the Office of Policy Development, was basically responsible for reviewing economic and domestic policy. In retrospect, I think it really should have been called the Office of Policy Implementation, because that is what we did.

Anderson points to the beneficial impact of this arrangement on Reagan's top domestic priority, economic policy:

[The staff] saw our job as keeping the policy effort focused on those things that President Reagan wanted done. We needed to control and channel and monitor a whole truckload of policies that we had already developed, and we had to do it in such a way that things got done in the order that Reagan wanted them done. We had to avoid starting new initiatives in sensitive, politically difficult policy areas.

We could choke off less important ideas and less relevant ideas that would have used up valuable time and manpower and prevented the President from achieving his key policy goals. That meant, for all practical purposes, at least during the first year or so, that we were focused tightly on economic policy and all other policies took a temporary back seat.

The Staff as Coordinators

The staffing of Reagan's Cabinet Councils, says Anderson, was carefully designed to keep the councils in sync with the President's objectives:

Each Cabinet Council was provided with a special support staff called a secretariat, and that secretariat had an executive secretary who ran it. Every Cabinet member of a council got to appoint one member, usually from his or her department, to the secretariat of the council.

This did a couple of things. When the secretariat met, it ensured that each Cabinet member would be fully informed of all actions taking place in their Cabinet councils. It also meant that the secretariat had a reliable, fast way to get information back to the Cabinet members. The executive secretaries of each Cabinet Council also all worked for the White House. In fact, they were all members of my staff, and they reported directly to me. So they had a dual role; they worked closely with the Cabinet members on the council, but they reported to me.

In addition, I appointed one or two, depending on the council, other White House staff members to each of the Cabinet Council secretariats. That was to ensure that there was a strong White House presence in all their deliberations. I had one main goal: to make sure that President Reagan's views were accurately and fully represented. And finally, as we developed these Cabinet Councils, a number of senior White House staff were named by the President to be actual members of each Cabinet Council. They included Ed Meese, Jim Baker, Michael Deaver, Vice President [George] Bush, and myself.

… So now you get the six Cabinet Councils, six secretariats, six executive secretaries. The executive secretaries, working through my office and Ed Meese's office, set the agenda of each Cabinet Council meeting, the time and the day of each meeting, and the place where the meetings would take place. And overseeing the whole thing were White House aides, senior aides. It was a management system that allowed them to shape and direct the course of policy discussion. They could place items on the agenda of the Cabinet Councils. They could remove items from the agenda of the Cabinet Councils. Or they could park items by sending them back for further review and discussion.

According to Anderson, the Reagan White House developed a layer below the Cabinet Councils to "hone policy and feed into the discussions of the Cabinet Council." These were referred to as "working groups":

These were all special groups established by the Cabinet Councils in conjunction with the Office of Policy Development and the council secretariats.

Whereas the secretariat of the council represented basically the Cabinet members, the working groups were essentially composed of experts in particular policy areas. For example, in economic policy or in the agricultural working group, whatever it was, the members of the working group could be drawn from any department throughout the government, any agency. And in some cases, these were private citizens. The criterion for membership in a working group was expertise in the policies under consideration.

Once these working groups were formed, at least one member of my White House staff in the Office of Policy Development was assigned to each and every working group to make sure once again that the views of President Reagan were represented faithfully. During the first year or so of the Reagan Administration, we used to have dozens of these working groups. I think the final total was 70 or 80, and the working groups reported to their respective Cabinet Councils and through the councils directly to the President.

During the first year or two of the Reagan Administration, they were particularly useful in diverting political attention away from dozens of issues clamoring for attention. It is surprising how many people who were on Reagan's White House staff initially had a whole bunch of new ideas they wanted to develop, and we were working on the economic policy. They had new ideas. We said fine. We set up a working group, and they went to work on it, and that allowed us to concentrate on completing what Reagan wanted done, which was the economic policy agenda.

Strong staff involvement and direction was essential for success. As veteran political reporter Bob Franken observes:

Martin Anderson [was] the man who wielded the two-by-four, the one who brought in the Cabinet members and said, "Here are your choices. Do as we say, or I am going to use this two-by-four on you." Tension is good, of course. I think everybody would agree that it is one of the underlying good things about our government, that you don't have people marching in lockstep. But I think any administration would feel that too much tension is not a good thing, and that is where Martin came in.

Although the senior staff played a critical "enforcer" role in keeping Cabinet government on track, Anderson is quick to point out that, as Reagan's chief domestic policy adviser, he was successful only because he conveyed the President's explicit wishes:

I would never tell a Cabinet person what to do. What I would do is say, "Here is what the President has said." In fact, one of the things we did during the transition is that we provided a nice looseleaf notebook, which was a summary of everything that President Reagan had said during the campaign, and in fact his whole life, on any issue that was going to come before them. They were called the "holy scrolls."

That was their marching orders. They weren't coming from me. They were coming from the President.

POLICYMAKING VEERING OFF TRACK

There are many ways that executive branch policymaking can get off track. White House drift, pressure from Congress, naiveté about the Cabinet, losing the big picture, and weak staffing can all contribute to a loss of momentum and lack of direction.

White House Drift

Even with a strong policymaking team in place, a President will encounter skepticism and policy disagreements from within his own White House, and this can undermine momentum and focus. According to Martin Anderson, the top Reagan aides sought to avoid such policy drift on economic issues by assembling a powerful group of outside experts, free from day-to-day political pressures, to bolster the President:

> We had a group of outside experts. At the time, we called it the President's Economic Policy Advisory Board. George Shultz was the chairman. Other members were Milton Friedman, Alan Greenspan, Arthur Burns, Paul McCracken, and Bill Simon. It was a "Who's Who" of extraordinary people with backgrounds in economics, had been in the government, who for one reason or another were not an official part of the Reagan Administration.

> Five times during that first year, when things got a little sticky inside, I put in a call to George Shultz, and George would call a meeting of the board. They would come in to town, and they would meet in the Roosevelt Room, and they would discuss economic policy. Then, at about 11 o'clock in the morning, the door would open up and President Reagan would walk in. He would look at them and smile, and go over and wink at Milton Friedman and pat Alan Greenspan on the shoulder and talk with Arthur Burns and joke with Shultz and then sit down.

> Don Regan was sitting there, and Murray Weidenbaum, and David Stockman, all very quiet. Basically [the outsiders] would tell Reagan two things. First of all, he was probably the greatest President since Abraham Lincoln; and second, what he was doing

was absolutely correct, and he should continue doing it. It was a very important thing to happen, because it straightened out the internal part of the White House staff also.

Pressure from Congress

The difficulty of keeping the President's Cabinet and senior agency team on track is not simply due to direct pressure from the bureaucracy and interest groups. Behind-the-scenes pressure from Members of Congress, often representing those same interests, can also thwart efforts to keep the Cabinet operating as a team. The strength of that pressure may reflect the balance of power in Washington. President Bush's Counsel, Boyden Gray, who also had served with Bush in the Reagan White House, saw the result of changes in congressional control:

C. Boyden Gray

> [We must remember] the iron triangle, the relationship of the various regulatory agencies and departments and the Congress, and how this triad plays out against the President. It was especially bad, I think, for President Bush when he faced a Democratic House and Senate. President Reagan had the luck, in part because he ran a good campaign in 1980, of having a Republican Senate for six of the first eight years. It is not a total coincidence that after he lost that Republican Senate, Iran–Contra again took over. That is a point which I think shouldn't get lost here.

Trying to block back-channel pressure is no easy task, as Gray found out:

> One of the initiatives that President Bush tried was to have the federal agencies, regulatory agencies, report *ex parte* contacts from Congressmen and their staff, just as they were required by informal precedent to report *ex parte* contacts by the business community or environmental groups at EPA [the Environmental Protection Agency]. And we suggested, merely suggested, that we would require the EPA or the Interior Department or this department or that department to report *ex parte* contacts by congressional staff. You have never seen such an

explosion, and, of course, the policy wasn't implemented.

Naiveté about the Cabinet

Success also requires the President to be realistic about his own Cabinet officers if he and the White House staff are to keep the Cabinet focused on his agenda. As Warshaw describes this process:

> Jimmy Carter is such a nice guy. He couldn't believe that his Cabinet officers weren't with him. He couldn't believe that his Cabinet officers would in any way turn to their departments and not inwards towards the White House staff.
>
> He had Stu Eizenstat handle the Domestic [Policy] Council system, and they did an okay job, not very aggressive. They really believed their Cabinet officers were okay. Well, as you remember, two years into that administration, Jimmy Carter fired half of his Cabinet officers because they were off in never-never land, going in their own direction. Bob Bergland would go over in the halls of Congress and lobby against the President. Can you imagine a Cabinet Secretary lobbying against the President of the United States?

According to Warshaw, George Bush exhibited a similar naiveté:

> George Bush put a lot of his friends into the Cabinet. And he couldn't believe that his friends would betray him, so he gave his friends lots of leeway in managing their own departments. There are a lot of problems with this.

Lack of a Clear Big Picture

More recently, President Clinton also lost the opportunity to have focused decision-making in his Cabinet. According to Warshaw, however, this had a rather different cause:

> Clinton very clearly realized that you need to deal with this co-option problem. You need to deal with the marrying-the-natives problem. So rather than having these constant regular sort of formal meetings with his Cabinet, what Bill Clinton has done is have these so-called advocacy groups.
>
> He brings them in, little groups of people, two and three here and there, based on issues, very tiny little issues. So if they are dealing with the Boston subway problem, the MTA, then he brings in a few people that may be familiar with that. It doesn't become a

broad issue. He doesn't deal with things as the Reagan Administration did: Everything they did, this is part of the big picture; and they kept reinforcing to the Cabinet officers, this is the big picture, and everything you and the departments do has to fit around it.

Bill Clinton never did that, partly because, like George Bush, he had some faith in his Cabinet officers, but there is a lot of pressure on the Cabinet officers. So the Cabinet Council structure that was created by John Ehrlichman, and a little bit by Daniel Patrick Moynihan, in the Nixon Administration was really brought to its highest level in the Reagan Administration, where you constantly bring in the Cabinet officers and reinforce them and tell them they are part of the presidential orbit: "We like you."

… The Clinton people haven't quite figured out—and that is one of the problems—that you need to not only network your own people. Washington is a big place. Hugh Hecklo once called it a government of strangers. It is still a government of strangers. Cabinet officers are often strangers. We need in the White House to find ways to mitigate the problems of being strangers, and the Cabinet Council system did that

So it was a brilliant system, and every administration has followed it in some way, shape, or form. But it is really Martin Anderson that perfected it.

Too Many Staff, Too Many Priorities

Other administrations' experiences demonstrate that firm staff leadership and a hardheaded presidential attitude are necessary if the Cabinet and Cabinet Councils are to be effective tools for turning the President's agenda into policy. President Ford, for example, suffered from weak staff control over the Domestic Council. Explains Shirley Warshaw:

Jerry Ford came in, and [Vice President Nelson Rockefeller named] Jim Cannon from *Time* magazine [to handle] the Domestic [Policy] Council. Well, Jim wasn't really a politician, and he had Rockefeller fighting with [Deputy Chief of Staff, and later Chief of Staff, Richard] Cheney and Cheney aligned with Ford, and poor Rockefeller and Cannon got lost. So the Ford Administration never really moved forward, although they tried to, on the Domestic Council concept.

Although the White House staff is critical to successful policy development, it does not follow that it is better. In fact, suggests Brookings Institution government expert Paul Light, the mushrooming of eager staff and working groups in recent years may have reduced both the quality and quantity of major policy initiatives:

> Why is it that, in the domestic policy process, Presidents have never had more help, the process itself is more formalized and structured than it has ever been in history, yet we are producing less and less by way of significant presidential policy.... [There is] the possibility that the more help we give the President inside the White House to make policy decisions, the smaller the decisions are.
>
> I'll give you just three little facts about the White House policy process today. Number one, there have never been more titled White House staffers in history. By that, I mean that the number of "free radical" staffers with no title except special assistant or counselor has declined dramatically over the last 30 years, so that everybody not only is a special assistant, but is a special assistant *for*. That is an interesting phenomenon.
>
> Number two, we have never had more units within the White House. Shirley [Warshaw] has done this wonderful work. If you read her book, *The Domestic Presidency*, it is one chart after another, and over time, the charts become denser and denser with new units. This administration added the new unit, the National Economic
> Council.
>
> Congress just approved, last year, a chief financial officer for the White House—for the White House, not for government generally....We have more and more accretion of offices within the White House to which a President can turn.
>
> Finally, we have more layers of help in the White House. When you were in the White House in 1976, 1980, you had an OMB director and a deputy director, and then you could get right down into the agency. Today at OMB, you have a director, a deputy director, a deputy director for management, and a set of associate directors, a set of assistant associate directors, deputy associate directors. You go all the way down through OMB, and it is more and more people who are doing stuff with titles, layers, and so forth.
>
> Is this a puzzle, then, that we can solve: more help for the President, more structure, more rules, more

procedures, tinier and tinier policies? I just offer that as a provoking causal hypothesis. It could be that, actually, the reason we have tinier policies and the reason we have more help for the President is that in fact there is a third hand working here.

Contrasting the Reagan and Clinton Administrations, Warshaw elaborates on Light's hypothesis by arguing that the fatal step for a White House is to combine too many "priorities" with too many staff members:

> The Reagan Administration was successful because it had phenomenal people, people that worked very, very well with President Reagan. They knew President Reagan. They understood his goals and objectives. You cannot overestimate the power of that, of these personal relationships.
>
> They also had a limited agenda, and moving a limited agenda forward is always easier than moving a broad agenda forward. The Clinton Administration has layer after layer, this broad number of policies. It is, of course, hurting them.
>
> The last time I counted, the Clinton Administration had 26 senior staff people with the title Assistant to the President. As you all know, "Assistant to the President" means those key people that came out of the Roosevelt Administration, when they were called administrative assistants, those six original people. They lost the word "administrative" and call them assistants to the President now. So if you have the title assistant to the President, you are a bigwig in the White House.
>
> Well, all of those people have staffs under them. So what we have seen, obviously, is the proliferation of the White House staff.
>
> When Martin Anderson was there, I remember he had about 11 senior staff people with the title Assistant to the President. So we have almost tripled. It is a huge increase. This increases the access points for all of these interest groups into the White House, and when you increase the access points, you increase the number of policies that are going to be considered.
>
> And Anderson was able to limit the number of people that had access to him, to limit the issues that came before senior staff meetings. That is much more difficult when you have 26 senior staff people, an untold number of special assistants who are also access points into the White House. You see this proliferation of ideas into the White House policy development structure, and that has been a big problem with this White House.

PARTICIPANTS

Enacting a National Security Agenda
February 23, 2000
St. Regis Hotel
Washington, D.C.

KIM R. HOLMES
Vice President and Director, The Kathryn and Shelby Cullom Davis Institute for International Studies

Presenters

ZBIGNIEW BRZEZINSKI
Former National Security Adviser to President Jimmy Carter

CASPAR WEINBERGER
Former Secretary of Defense to President Ronald Reagan

Commentators

HELLE BERING
Editor of the Editorial Page, The Washington Times

ROBERT KAGAN
Carnegie Endowment for International Peace

CHARLES KRAUTHAMMER
Syndicated Columnist

PETER RODMAN
Former Deputy Assistant to President Ronald Reagan for National Security Affairs

FAREED ZAKARIA
Managing Editor, Foreign Affairs

Chapter V:
Enacting a
National Security Agenda

"If there is going to be a new foreign policy by a new administration, it will have to begin with a vision, and it will have to be sold to the American people."
—Charles Krauthammer

From the founding of the American republic until the middle of the 20th century, Presidents formulated and conducted the nation's foreign, defense, and national security policies through the Secretaries of State and War. After World War II, with passage of the National Security Act of 1947, the White House began to exert greater control over the nation's security policies. The legislation put the military services under a new umbrella, the Department of Defense, created the Central Intelligence Agency (CIA) out of the wartime Office of Strategic Services, and established the National Security Council (NSC).

The NSC's intended purpose was to "advise the President with respect to the integration of domestic, foreign, and military policies related to the nation's security" and to compel the President to consult regularly with military experts. In recent years, the term "security" has expanded to include economic and trade issues, energy dependence, globalization, and other matters.

President Harry S. Truman used the NSC as international situations warranted. Truman's successor, Dwight D. Eisenhower, incorporated it fully into his decision-making apparatus, upgrading the position of Executive Director to Special Assistant for National Security. Eisenhower also used the NSC as he did his Cabinet; that is, as a deliberative body that assembled all parties with an interest in a particular matter to air and resolve differences. In naming banker Robert Cutler to head this operation, Eisenhower established a precedent: The NSC director functioned as a coordinator rather than as a policymaker.

Under President John F. Kennedy, NSC director McGeorge Bundy operated as an advocate and operative rather than as a facilitator of opposing viewpoints. This shift resulted primarily from presidential impatience with the bureaucratic slowness, lethargy, and reluctance to provide clear and concise policy recommendations during the Cold War on the part of the State Department and other agencies. In addition, Kennedy believed that he had been misled by government professionals during the Bay of Pigs crisis.

The pattern established under President Kennedy continued under Richard Nixon, with National Security Adviser Henry Kissinger operating his own bureaucracy, enabling him to develop and often implement policy independently of the State Department.

Since Nixon, Presidents have tried to strike a balance in advice they received from the NSC, the State Department, the Defense Department, the Joint Chiefs of Staff (JCS), the CIA, and other entities. When NSC officials took actions that were contrary to the wishes of the Secretary of State or the Secretary of Defense, or that were without explicit presidential authorization, unwanted attention was paid to the NSC's operations, spurring reforms.

The end of the Cold War has presented new, unanticipated challenges both to a President's ability to conduct foreign policy and to the ability of the United States to act unilaterally. The United States must now, more than ever before, consult with other nations due to international agreements and globalization, increased military intervention as part of international peacekeeping and other operations, the fraying of old alliances in the absence of a clear threat, and the decline of the President's standing. The President is no longer the principal actor in the international arena; he is instead the preeminent player on a team that often includes foreign governments, Congress, the media, and state and local governments.

NATIONAL SECURITY AND THE NATURE OF THE PRESIDENCY

The modern presidency has been shaped by the three seminal experiences of the 20th century: the Great Depression, World War II, and the Cold War. The powers of the presidency were expanded by President Franklin D. Roosevelt, first as a response to the Depression, and then later as a wartime measure during World War II. The President's powers were further expanded after the advent of the Cold War. The demands of a growing superpower, the most important of which was the need to manage nuclear weaponry and a global set of military alliances, created a national security state. At the top of this superpower presided the American President, whose powers and privileges greatly exceeded those of any previous President.

The end of the Cold War has created a debate not only over the nature of American national security interests and strategy, but also over the nature of the presidency. The question naturally arose: Should the presidency itself change now that the demands of the Cold War are over? This question is important because it goes to the heart of the next President's attitude toward both national security strategy and the organizational apparatus to implement it.

Fareed Zakaria, Managing Editor of *Foreign Affairs*, has said that the end of the Cold War fundamentally changed the presidency. What once was a privileged position became a position that once again had to compete with reemerging actors. As Zakaria says, the Depression, World War II, and the Cold War combined "to create a 'national security state' and to privilege the President as the national spokesman, bureaucratically far above other leaders within society and the government in general." This situation, however, began to change in 1989.

Fareed Zakaria

Congress was the first to reemerge as a challenge to presidential dominance. The second major player, notes Zakaria, is the states. As he says, "a second and somewhat less remarked upon change has been the rising power of the states ... [which] have asserted prerogatives about the central government that would have been unthinkable during the Cold War." He points to the recent refusal by the Governor of Virginia to accept a request from the Secretary of State, and then from President Clinton, to abide by certain treaty obligations with regard to the arrest of a foreign national.

The third challenge to the centrality of presidential authority, notes Zakaria, is the rising influence of non-governmental organizations (NGOs) on U.S. national security policy:

> The number of NGOs that have grown and that have been started in the last 10 years is triple what it was 10 years ago. This trend is likely to continue because, as in business, there are now dramatically lower costs to entry into the NGO world.

The attention given to NGOs demonstrates both their growing influence and their savvy use of technology to focus attention on an issue. Looking at the 1999 demonstrations against the World Trade Organization in Seattle, Zakaria observed that many of the groups "quoted on CNN and MSNBC ... were three people and a fax machine" and that this trend" was

Charles Krauthammer

"likely to continue because you will get down to the point where it might even be no real organization, just a powerful e-mail-blasting system within a server."

The Gulf War, Zakaria argues, reflected the changed circumstances for presidential leadership and foreshadowed future decision-making by the commander in chief under the influence of various actors:

> In opposing Iraq's conquest of Kuwait, President Bush felt it necessary to use the United Nations to get Iraq condemned as an aggressor, the underlying legal basis for Operation Desert Storm. He also felt it necessary to engage other regional and international actors to gain broad legitimacy for the operation to remove Iraqi forces from Kuwait.

Yet Charles Krauthammer, a syndicated columnist, offers a contrary view of the presidency. He believes that the presidency has been "miniaturized" during the past eight years, reflecting changing historical circumstances:

> With the end of the Cold War, [the United States has] been so obviously dominant we haven't had the kind of crises and challenges that characterized the 60 years before that. We haven't needed a great President, an FDR or a Churchill, and we haven't had one with any inclination to act as an FDR or a Churchill.

While Zakaria argues that the emergence of Congress to restrain presidential power is a new phenomenon, Krauthammer believes that the President is still the dominant player. Even with the attention focused on Newt Gingrich's Republican Revolution of 1994, Krauthammer says:

> It turns out that in the modern era, in the media age, a President can dominate the political stage in a way that is simply impossible for a disparate congressional leadership, even one as flush with victory and for a time united as were the Republicans.

In fact, argues Krauthammer, Congress "hasn't had a role at all in the Clinton era [comparable to] the role of the Democratic opposition in the debates on Nicaragua, El Salvador, on Euromissiles—on the Pershings—on the whole structure of the Cold War struggle" as it did in the 1970s and 1980s:

> Compare how powerful and important the Democrats were. I'm leaving out here the Vietnam War era, of course, where Congress was able to entirely undermine a President's policy. Compare that with how ineffectual has been any opposition by Congress to foreign policy as waged by the Administration over the last eight years.

Krauthammer's assessment is shared by former Reagan Administration official Robert Kagan. Pointing to President Bill Clinton's decision to intervene in Kosovo, Kagan notes that "Congress was against Kosovo. It was totally against Kosovo, and [President Clinton] did it anyway without the smallest difficulty."

VISION, PRIORITIES, AND STRATEGY

The changing international environment and the vision, priorities, and strategies adopted by a particular President will shape the nature and role of the presidency. How the President conceives of America's role in the world, and whether a President chooses to focus mainly on domestic or foreign priorities, will determine the leadership style and content of national security policy. The organization, management style, and personnel choices of the administration will reflect the President's vision for America's international role. While the President's vision is open to debate, it does not obviate the importance of these choices. Instead, it accentuates the importance of understanding the President's vision for America's role in the world.

Presidential Vision and America's Role in the World

The President's vision of America's international role is critical to the structure and management of national security policy. In fact, concludes Krauthammer, the President must use his vision of America's role in the world as a starting point for a coherent policy strategy:

> In thinking about how to structure and organize the policy of a new administration, [the President] must

start with what a former President once called the "vision thing." ... It would be very important for a President to be able to, apart from the structure of those who serve under him, and apart from his relations with allies and the military and Congress, to have a vision if he is going to conduct an effective foreign policy. If there is going to be a new foreign policy by a new administration, it will have to begin with a vision, and it will have to be sold to the American people.

Krauthammer goes on to argue that two competing world-views have emerged in the post-Cold War era, a liberal view and a conservative view. The next President, he says, will reflect one of these two visions or represent some blend of the two. The liberal vision has three basic tenets: "universalism, a sense that it is international institutions which ought to be the focus of American policy; legalism, an enormous emphasis on treaties, agreements, on parchment; and lastly, on humanitarianism, America acting as a benefactor all around the globe." The ultimate liberal objective is the creation of "a kind of global, international community."

The conservative vision, on the other hand, does not rest on the United Nations or abstract legalism. Rather it represents a "a nationalist foreign policy rooted in the understanding that what keeps international stability is ... American power first and last," with the complementary understanding "that America ought to conserve stability and serve the world by advancing its own national interest as opposed to trying to create a kind of global, international community."

Robert Kagan, however, does not see a major difference between the foreign policy philosophies of the Democrat and Republican parties: "The nation has the character it has. There is only so much you can do to reorient the functional feelings that the nation has."

Instead, Kagan believes that what separates the two parties is "a nationalism issue." For instance, he says that the Republican presidential candidates represent—although it may seem paradoxical—"internationalist nationalists." Thus, they support the notion that American "nationalism is about universal ideas." While there is no clear definition of the meaning of nationalism, Kagan argues:

It's not a blood-and-soil nationalism. It's not the Fatherland-type nationalism. [Instead] there is an inherent international view in our nationalism.... The most successful American Presidents who happened in the century ... and I'm thinking particularly of Roosevelt and Reagan, essentially married an appeal to nationalism with an appeal to the idea that

that nationalism means that the United States has a role to play in the world.

In Kagan's assessment, this "international nationalist" wing of the Republican Party dominates the party, or, at least, this approach rules among those who vie for the Oval Office. A different strain of nationalism, however, has emerged in the Republican-led Congress:

> The other strain, which is more located in Congress, is a more insular nationalism, which I think is closer in its sensibility to almost a blood-and-soil nationalism because it's also married up in certain cases with concerns about immigration, with concerns about multiculturalism, which may or may not be justified.

This nationalism, however, is subject to change. Kagan believes that if a Republican wins the presidency, the hesitancy on the part of Congress to intervene will vanish. As he says:

> My guess is Congress is going to flip around. Republicans who have been more restrained and looking toward a more minimal foreign policy are probably going to follow the direction of the Republican President, who is going to be more internationalist.

Kagan believes the Democrats will also change positions as well, moving away from their support for President Clinton's interventions:

> The Democrats will go back to their earlier, more isolationist incarnation. I predict that the next Republican President is going to get involved in one of these quasi-humanitarian, quasi-national-interest interventions with substantial support in the Republican Congress and almost total opposition from Democrats in the Congress.

POLICY PRIORITIES: NATIONAL SECURITY VERSUS DOMESTIC POLICY

A President must decide early whether national security and foreign policy are a high or low priority—and this decision will affect the President's vision and strategy. Former Secretary of Defense Caspar Weinberger and former National Security Adviser Zbigniew Brzezinski both agree that the President must determine the priority to be given to foreign policy. From this determination will follow decisions on personnel and organizational structure. As Weinberger notes, "in order to organize an administration for national security ... you have to have, first of all, a decision by the administration as to what it wants to accomplish in foreign policy."

Policy Prioritization and Personnel

Weinberger observes that a President who "accepts the fact that we need to play a leadership role in the future ... will have a quite different organization and quite different personnel than if the goal is to be re-elected." But this distinction is not the only concern in selecting the personnel responsible for the implementation of national security policy. Brzezinski's experience leads him

to conclude that "Presidents who put a higher emphasis on domestic policy tend to lean heavily on Secretaries of State who are dominant [while] Presidents who see themselves as architects of foreign policy tend to lean more heavily on their National

Zbigniew Brzezinski and Caspar Weinberger

Security Advisers." In the latter case, the National Security Adviser becomes "the bureaucratic beneficiary of presidential reliance on that close relationship."

From these observations, Weinberger agrees with Brzezinski's remark that:

> The President really needs to reflect how he is going to use his time and where his priorities are going to be and choose his key advisors on that basis ... a President who is not really interested in foreign policy should make a very deliberate effort to choose a Secretary of State who is going to play a preeminent role; [but] if he thinks otherwise, then he should choose someone who is more of a luminary and put more emphasis on the office of the National Security Adviser.

The President's priorities even affect the national security apparatus he will establish. Brzezinski continues:

> In that connection, I think the President also must give some thought to what kind of a national security system he desires. In making that system, he should ask himself whether it helps the foreign policy coordination process to impose direct presidential control.

THE TRANSITION

The electoral campaign and the transition process influence the prioritization of issues and provide an indication of a President's focus once elected. Brzezinski notes that the transition process usually distinguishes between those "Presidents who put primary emphasis on foreign policy in the definition of their role and in their sense of historical responsibility, and [those] Presidents who will put more of an emphasis on domestic politics." This prioritization "immediately tends to affect how they operate and the kind of choices they make." Brzezinski adds:

> The electoral campaign [however] is not necessarily a good guide in making this determination, because an electoral campaign is designed to win the elections, and that may not tell us too much about a new President. It certainly doesn't tell us much about the major foci of his foreign policy because a presidential campaign distorts foreign policy. It tends to primitivize foreign policy, reducing it to simple black-and-white issues.

Yet before a President can enact his vision, he must first take over the machinery of government. To be successful, the candidate must make a smooth transition from campaigning to governing. This requires serious and early planning. All too often, Presidents arrive in Washington woefully unprepared for the task of leading the nation. Long before they and their teams enter the White House, careful planning must be completed, and specific steps must be taken to prepare the way for a successful presidency.

Brzezinski notes that it is important to focus the attention of the transition teams on the purposes and goals of the administration:

> One of the problems over the years has been that transition teams tend to be formed very quickly, without much advance thought regarding these questions. Transition teams necessarily are staffed by people who are aspirants to jobs and are often focused on securing a position in the new administration rather than answering the critical questions that the President and his closest associates may have. Hence, the choice of a transition team ought to be made very clearly with these larger questions in mind. Otherwise, a transition team can become a source of confusion or simply self-promotion rather than serving the interests and the choices that the new President-elect ought very consciously to make.

Weinberger, using the Reagan experience, emphasizes that presidential campaigns need to start transition planning early:

> Transition planning started very early. Without an overriding position … you're going to have confusion, and then you're going to have a reflection of that not only in the people who have been chosen, but in the bureaucracy that is expected to carry out the orders.

Washington Times editorial page editor Helle Bering also notes the importance of starting early with transition teams. She describes the historical experiences of the Reagan and Clinton Administrations:

> The Clinton team did the exact opposite of what the Reagan people did. [The Clinton team] waited until the last minute, and then they acted out of complete chaos in the months of December and January, whereas if you go back to 1980, already after Reagan had won New Hampshire, he started putting together his foreign policy and domestic policy agendas and teams, and they started acting as early as February, which made for a huge difference.

The lack of preparedness on the part of the Clinton team was responsible for much of the confusion in Clinton's foreign policy. As Bering notes:

> When the Clinton team came in, all they could do was say that there was no daylight between them and the Bush Administration. There was no vision. There was no sense of purpose, and that soon evolved into the grasping onto the United Nations as the saving life raft for their foreign policy, which was not a particularly good idea, whereas with the Reagan people you had a strong sense of purpose.

Reagan, prior to taking office, had a clear idea of where he wanted to take the country. Weinberger describes how policy dominated the discussions of the transition teams for President Reagan:

> The important thing is to have a very clear policy, and it seemed to me that those discussions that we had prior to the inauguration of President Reagan set the stage to a very considerable extent for the policies that he was going to follow.

ORGANIZING NATIONAL SECURITY POLICYMAKING

There are many facets to organizing the apparatus for national security policymaking. Once the President decides whether national security will be a priority, he can decide not only what kind of people he wants in the Cabinet, but also how to apportion power and influence among the various agencies and offices involved in the making of national security policy. The workings of the government—both its limitations and its possibilities—must be fully understood before it can be properly utilized. The inter-agency process should be orga-

Helle Bering

nized to reflect the President's goals, priorities, and style of leadership. The organization of the national security apparatus should not be left to chance or even tradition, but should be consciously adapted to achieve the President's agenda.

Zbigniew Brzezinski supplies a list of the questions the President must answer in organizing a national security system:

> Does he see the national security system essentially as a coordinating function providing him with analysis to enlighten his understanding and to facilitate some of his choices? Is the national security system designed to overcome the inherent inclination of large bureaucracies to be overly cautious and not particularly innovative? And does the national security system spur new policies and produce initiatives?

The answers the President provides to these questions will help him decide on the structure of national security agencies and processes. Brzezinski continues:

> Closely connected with this issue is the whole question of how actually to structure the decision-making process. Every President shortly after the assumption of office issues an order structuring his decision-making system, in fact, very deliberately—frankly, out of political and personal ego—renaming the key steps for the documents that are going to be issued in the President's name, the names of committees, and so forth.

> That is an extremely important component of the transition process, for it sets in motion the necessary decision-making dynamics and the process very early on. A President has to be very conscious of the fact that the manner in which he proceeds will ultimately determine how his system will be structured.

A President should decide on the structure and organization of the policymaking apparatus prior to taking office, because the consequences of inattention to these decision-making details can be troublesome. As Brzezinski points out, "Slight degrees of emphasis, small shades of difference, or even minor sources of confusion in setting up the process can have a long-term impact on the ability to operate."

Indeed, the President should have documents outlining the structure of government ready on the day he takes office. Brzezinski concludes:

> The key document describing the proposed restructuring should be produced quickly, preferably on the first or second day of the new administration, so as to ensure that it doesn't become an object of bureaucratic struggle.

The President's Relationship with the Director of Central Intelligence and the National Security Adviser

One of the President's most important decisions, Brzezinski argues, is structuring the relationship of the President to the National Security Adviser and the Director of Central Intelligence (DCI). Brzezinski says:

> There is the problem of how you organize larger scale planning in the government, and that planning process in the U.S. government is very messy and has been that way for years. There is a specific problem of the role of the CIA and the Director's access to the President.

> The Director of Central Intelligence (DCI) typically desires direct access to the President. ... Clearly the DCI must be involved in the NSC process, and there should indeed be some access. Whether he should brief the President every day, however, is an open question. Over the years, a tendency has developed for the National Security Adviser to fill this role rather than the Director, in part because the President, in being briefed, does not want to deal with the head of a huge agency which then gets feedback from the briefing.

> Moreover, the President also wants to be able to use the briefing to sharpen his understanding of the immediate policy issues that he faces, and in so doing he needs some interaction with a person that's close to him and can give him advice and can refine the analysis that he is getting. The Director of Central Intelligence cannot do that. It has to be someone close to the President.

Hence, I would emphasize the unique role of the National Security Adviser because he alone can say: "Look, in the next three days you have to make the following three decisions. Here is the way the Secretary of State and the Secretary of Defense disagree. Here is the input from the JCS and the CIA, and these are the ramifications of your decision."

Then the President can say: "Well, Joe, what do you think, since I trust your judgment? If I didn't, you wouldn't be here." I don't think the President can have that kind of an interaction with the DCI.

The President's Relationship with the Military

Another important concern is the President's relationship with the armed forces. Brzezinski argues:

Obviously, the Secretary of Defense is critically important and a broadly significant player in the national security process. This begs the question of whether the President should have a direct relationship with the Chairman of the JCS, and how the President makes sure that what the Secretary of Defense tells him corresponds with what the Chairman of the JCS thinks, and vice versa.

Obviously within the Department of Defense structure, the Chairman of the JCS cannot undermine the Secretary of Defense. At the same time, however, the military perspective is very important, and sometimes even politically sensitive. Hence, some sort of a direct, carefully structured relationship between the President and the JCS chairman is necessary while keeping the line of command hierarchically clean.

Cap Weinberger agrees that the President must bring in the military early for national security planning, not only because of its expertise, but also because the military's support will be needed to enact the President's program. Weinberger contends that there must be recognition of the military's major role:

By this, I don't mean trying to politicize the military or bring them in support of an individual or a party. This would be about the worst thing anybody could do. Rather, I mean gaining an understanding among the people who are senior in the military who either are or are likely to be a part of the Joint Chiefs of Staff as to what it is that this incoming administration wants to accomplish. It is important not to start with a blank page on January 20.

Bipartisanship

Brzezinski argues that it is important to strive for bipartisanship in national security because it is one of the keys to enacting a successful national security program. He says:

> The new President from the new party in power has to make a very serious effort early on to set in motion some structured process to create bipartisanship in foreign policy. This is crucial, and it tends to be neglected.

> I would hope that a new President would reach out and have a bipartisan effort not only in terms of rhetoric and outreach, but in terms of appointments.

GETTING THE RIGHT PEOPLE

One factor critical to the successful enactment of the President's national security agenda is getting the right people—people who believe in the President and his program, and people the President trusts. However, before the President can know which people to choose, he must know what he wants to accomplish. People and policy are intrinsically linked. Brzezinski makes this point clear:

> The President has to have some self-conscious understanding of the role he wants to play, particularly with regard to foreign policy because there are significant, even very nuanced, differences between different kinds of roles the President can play.

> A President ought to determine on the basis of that involvement where he places the people that he wants to work with him. A President may choose a different kind of a person to be Secretary of State and a different kind of person to be National Security Adviser. That choice is very sensitive and very critical. Then, having made that choice, he goes on to the process.

> The process has to be consistent with the choices he has already made. If the process is to maximize the central role of the President and the concentration of decision-making in the White House, then obviously you make arrangements which enhance the role of the NSC. If you want the State Department to be dominant, if you are not going to be deeply involved, but you have a sense of direction, then you choose a person who can provide continuity and a general sense of direction from State. One must make this decision with the knowledge, however, that you are not going to get very much inno-

vation because inevitably the Secretary of State becomes a prisoner of the bureaucratic machinery.

So it starts really with the President, goes from the President to his people, and then to the process. The three have to be closely related.

Brzezinski notes that time is critical to this part of the process, arguing that the President-elect should make "basic choices at the beginning of December so that [his] transition teams reflect those choices and don't complicate the process. And [he] ought to have people in place and a presidential order ready by the last week of January."

Weinberger believes that it is critically important for the President to hire people who share his vision of the world, noting that:

They might not necessarily be representatives of various wings of the party. They might not necessarily be people who had a geographic balance. They might not necessarily be people who would help in getting an administration re-elected.

Weinberger sees the campaign as an important mechanism for vetting and choosing the President's national security team: "People should be chosen for their capabilities in presenting the foreign policy program of the candidate during the campaign." Those who can skillfully articulate and defend the candidate's foreign policy positions "could fall rather naturally into the role of helping to carry out the policies and the plans of the new administration."

THE NATIONAL SECURITY BUREAUCRACY

Sometimes, however, having the right people is not enough. Former Reagan Administration Deputy Assistant to the President for National Security Affairs Peter Rodman describes how President Nixon's loyal national security team faced a hostile bureaucracy in the State Department:

Nixon pulled the reins of power into the White House, and the National Security Adviser and his office was given the chair of the some of these key committees [formerly chaired by the State Department]. This at the time was thought of as a great coup d'etat.

Rodman notes that "most recent administrations have adopted more or less the same bureaucratic structure," but that "what really led Nixon to pull the reins of power into the White House in such a systematic way was the fact that the State Department seemed willfully to misunderstand the foreign policy that he wanted to conduct." Rodman describes how this process worked with respect to Nixon's policy toward the Soviet Union:

> Nixon came in with a very definite idea that he
> wanted to link arms control with other aspects of
> Soviet policy. He didn't want to start arms control
> negotiations right away. [Rather] he wanted to for-
> mulate a defense strategy within which negotiations
> on arms control would have a place.
>
> He sent messages, both orally and in writing ... to
> his Cabinet departments that this is how he wanted
> to proceed. But, again, the State Department was
> negotiating with the Russians almost immediately
> on setting a date for arms control and this and that
> because obviously the State Department, and to
> some degree even the Defense Department, were
> much more responsive to media pressures and con-
> gressional pressures than they were to presidential
> authority.

Kagan describes how Secretary of State James Baker had a similar distrust of the State Department bureaucracy:

> The Bush Administration decided that George
> Shultz had been captured by the State Department
> and therefore tried to concentrate power in three or
> four people around the Secretary of State. [I]n some
> cases that was beneficial, but in some cases that
> meant that things kept biting them that they didn't
> see coming around the corner. They were constantly
> being surprised by events and crises.

The issue, according to Kagan, is not the expertise of the falli-
ble bureaucracy. Instead, it is the structure that exists under the
Secretary that matters. If there were "powerful assistant secretaries watching all of these problems ... there would be fewer sur-
prises." As Kagan notes:

> The Reagan Administration had very powerful assis-
> tant secretaries, not only in the State Department,
> but also in the Defense Department. You've got peo-
> ple like Richard Perle and Rich Armitage in the
> Defense Department. You've got Elliott Abrams and
> Paul Wolfowitz and Peter Rodman in the State
> Department. And I think that one of the things that
> that determined was that it's not that hard to grasp
> hold of the bureaucracy if you put your people in at
> that operational level. Strong, politically appointed
> assistant secretaries bend very quickly their bureaus
> to their will.

Weinberger also doubts that the foreign policy bureaucracy is
ungovernable. Rather, he believes that the President can make the
bureaucracies of the State Department and the Defense Department reflect his will:

Bureaucracy basically will do what it is asked to do. They are very loyal. They are very dependable. They are very expert. But they have to know what the policy is; otherwise, they will either do nothing, they will formulate it themselves, or there will be an enormous amount of confusion as a result. So it goes back to the President, what he wants to do and how early he impresses his appointees with that.

SELECTING THE CABINET SECRETARY

Before the President can mobilize the bureaucracy behind his program, he must choose a Cabinet that believes in his program. The President must find Cabinet officers who will faithfully carry out his program. Loyalty to the President, and not the Cabinet agency, is key. As Rodman points out:

Cabinet officers have to decide whether they are the President's representative in the bureaucracy. Is it their job to represent the President's will and to impose the President's wishes on the bureaucracy, or, alternatively, are they the representative of the bureaucracy in the Cabinet?

Are they just going to reflect the pressures their agencies are feeling all of the time from Congress and the media? If all they are is the bureaucracy's representative in the presidential councils, all they are is another pressure group on the President rather than an ally or an arm of presidential authority.

Even if the President has a loyal team, he still must lead his national security and foreign policy teams and give his programs coherence and direction. As Rodman emphasizes:

Coherence can only come from the President under any procedure. If the President has strong convictions and a vision and a sense of what our strategy should be, then one way or the other he is going to try to impose his coherence and discipline on the government. Ideally, he should do it through clear authority and direction to Cabinet officers who are responsive to his leadership; but I can assure you that if it doesn't happen, then the President ... will find his own ways of giving effect to his wishes, even if the rest of the government is not totally responsive.

GAINING SUPPORT FOR
THE PRESIDENT'S PROGRAM

No new President starts his term with a "fresh slate" when it comes to devising and implementing a national security agenda. The long-term security interests of the nation, the commitments of prior administrations, and the statutory requirements imposed by Congress influence the policies of every new President. Nevertheless, a newly elected President can take steps to ensure his administration devises and imposes policies that conform to his vision of the role the United States will play in world events and its security needs.

To succeed, the new President must decide on the emphasis he wishes to place on foreign affairs, and put in place a structure that reflect his priorities. He must also display an understanding of his ability to maneuver in a highly changing international environment, and an appreciation of how actions taken in one part of the world can influence outcomes in others and how his foreign policy apparatus can shape policies. He must devise a system for selecting the persons best able to help him translate his vision into reality.

As daunting as this job may be, Presidents need not be alone when making these decisions. Able veterans from past administrations are available to provide advice and impart the benefits of their experience. Distilling the best of their advice has become a common practice for each administration since the end of World War II. The advice of foreign policy experts helped produce policies that ultimately ended the Cold War, and it could help point the way to a new consensus of what American foreign policy in the future.

Caspar Weinberger emphasizes the importance of early planning in selling the President's program. Even before the inauguration, the President should be meeting with key members of Congress to gain their support. Key opinion leaders in the foreign policy field should be identified and, if possible, brought into the campaign. If they cannot be actual campaign advisers or surrogate speakers, then they should be members of outreach organizations. Finally, the staff should approach key members of the press to explain the President's agenda. The President should not wait until after the election to begin this outreach; all of these efforts should be accomplished during the campaign. Preparing to market the President's agenda should be one of the transition team's top priorities.

Furthermore, Weinberger believes, the President should establish contact early with America's key allies before and soon after the inauguration. They need to understand his agenda and be encouraged to support it. If the President works closely with America's allies as early as possible, he may be able to avoid misunderstandings and even crises later in his term.

Dealing with National Security Crises

More than any other issue, national security crises stress the presidency and reveal weaknesses in character, leadership, and organization. If a President is unprepared for a crisis—if his vision is blurred or his team divided—then the nation can be seriously threatened. Crises can shape and alter the course of a presidency, as the Bay of Pigs and Berlin Wall crises did for John F. Kennedy's Administration. And, of course, they can destroy a presidency, as the Iran hostage crisis did for Jimmy Carter. A President ignores crisis planning at his own peril.

Not all crises that affect national security have origins in foreign affairs. Weinberger describes how the air traffic control crisis in the first year of Reagan's presidency helped galvanize support for his presidency and, thereby, demonstrated his credibility and strength abroad. Weinberger says:

> One of the very early things in the Reagan Administration was the crisis caused by the air traffic control strike, which had the possibility of not only tying up civil aviation, but making all of the aerial activities of the country either come to a halt or be far more dangerous. How would he deal with this? He dealt with it very quickly and very completely. ... It was a very important thing not only in and of itself, but as a test, as a demonstration of the way the leadership would be exercised in the new administration.

A crisis consumes the President's time, which is extremely limited to begin with. Brzezinski believes that clarity of vision is vitally important to weathering a crisis: "If a President has a clear vision, then he is in a position to make a good judgment when a crisis occurs as to whether the crisis is a challenge to that vision or a diversion from it." Brzezinski continues:

> If the President has a sense of strategy or vision and a crisis arises, and he knows it's a challenge to his strategy, he will hopefully give it all of the necessary time and deal with it accordingly. If he doesn't, then I don't think he can decide whether it's a real challenge to his strategy or merely a diversion. Then he can fail to act, not realizing it's a challenge to his strategy, or he can overly engage himself in dealing with something that is not a serious crisis. I think the amount of time President Clinton spent on Haiti is a good example of this point.

Not all crises are to be feared, however. Sometimes a foreign crisis offers an opportunity to demonstrate resolve or accomplish a larger strategic goal. Kim R. Holmes, Vice President and Director of the Kathryn and Shelby Cullom Davis Institute for International Studies at The Heritage Foundation, contends:

In terms of the sense of a crisis being a challenge, how the President handles that can also turn it into an opportunity. I'm thinking about how President Reagan handled the whole Euromissile crisis, for example, which seemed at the time to be an assault on the entire Western alliance. But the way that German Chancellor Helmut Kohl and President Reagan handled that actually turned it into an important solidifying point for the alliance. It also demonstrated a larger commitment to overturn the challenge of the Soviet Union.

Charles Krauthammer agrees:

I think that the Reagan Administration brilliantly seized on the Euromissile crisis … [which] was the most understated, unappreciated victory in the Cold War. The Euromissile crisis was a threat to the alliance, and it ended up not only with the Soviets backing down, but disarming of the left with the Intermediate Range Nuclear Forces (INF) treaty. It accomplished two ends at once.

Krauthammer points to President Clinton's handling of Haiti as an example of how a crisis can become an emblem of a President's vision of foreign policy:

It may have begun as a distraction but I would argue that, in fact, it became the model or an emblem of what really is the foreign policy vision of the Clinton Administration. … Madeleine Albright, when she was sworn in as U.N. ambassador, spoke of her mission as being "to terminate the abominable injustices that still plague our civilization." That's a coherent vision: America's role in the world is to terminate abominable injustices. Haiti is one example. Getting more deeply involved in Somalia was a second. Bosnia, Kosovo, I think, are other examples.

Vision can also enable a President to define which crises merit his attention. The "CNN effect," in which television coverage dictates policy is often cited as a rule: "If CNN goes somewhere, the President ineluctably has to follow." Yet, as Zakaria believes, if the President has sufficient vision and resolve, he can not only shape the crisis, but also resist the manipulation by the press and his political opponents. According to Zakaria, it is not true that foreign policy is "a kind of hostage to some 24-year-old [producer] in Atlanta who decided to send a camera crew somewhere":

That just isn't the case, particularly in the post Cold War world in which the threats are more ambiguous. The President has an enormous ability to define what he sees as a crisis and what he sees as a threat. There is no evidence that continued television coverage of some issue forces the President's hand.

PARTICIPANTS

Working with Congress to Enact an Agenda
February 9, 2000
St. Regis Hotel
Washington, D.C.

Presenters

ALBERT AISELE
Editor, The Hill

PAT GRIFFIN
*Former Assistant to and Director of Legislative Affairs
for President Bill Clinton*

TOM KOROLOGOS
*Former Deputy Assistant for Senate Relations to
President Richard Nixon and President Gerald Ford*

JAMES A. THURBER
*Center for Congressional and Presidential Studies,
American University*

Commentators

GARY ANDRES
*Former Deputy Assistant to President George Bush
for Legislative Affairs*

RICHARD COHEN
Congressional Reporter, National Journal

HELEN DEWAR
Senate Reporter, The Washington Post

ED GILLESPIE
*Former Republican National Committee Director of Communica-
tions and
Congressional Affairs*

DONALD LAMBRO
Chief Political Correspondent, The Washington Times

Chapter VI:
Working with Congress to Enact an Agenda

"I think one of the toughest things that a President has to do, of either party, is to help explain to members of his own party where his interests are not exactly the same as his party's congressional interests."

—Pat Griffin

One of the major challenges faced by every President is how to move a program through Congress. For much of American history, conventional wisdom has held that a President's ability to transform policy recommendations into law is the key determinant of the success or failure of a presidency. Journalists who cover a President's administration, and historians who evaluate his place in history, all consider a President's legislative success in their assessments.

Presidents can do a great deal administratively to change how the government works and the direction in which it moves. Yet Presidents must still come before Congress—a co-equal branch of government—to enact lasting changes and secure funding for their requests. There are no roadmaps that tell Presidents how to succeed at transforming policy into law.

Nor is it clear that Presidents who once served in Congress are more likely to enjoy legislative success than those who have not. "Outsider" Ronald Reagan did rather well with his policies, as did "insider" Lyndon Johnson. Contrary to expectations, it is not always true that a President's programs sail easily through Congress when the same party controls Congress and the White House, as John Kennedy, Jimmy Carter, and Bill Clinton all learned.

Presidents are most able to gain congressional support for their programs early in their terms, when the election "mandate" is still fresh and they are still in their "honeymoon" period with Congress and the public. Presidents who make good first impressions on Capitol Hill and with the public usually achieve success.

Political pundits—and incoming Presidents themselves—have tended to hold new administrations to the standard of legislative achievement Franklin Roosevelt set in his first "100 days." Presidents can overcome their early mistakes, however, as they learn the legislative ropes and adjust to changing political landscapes. In some cases, Presidents can achieve a "victory" through negative actions such as an upheld veto, rather than by heroically pushing for programs with no chance of passage. At other times, Presidents may "win" by staking out a position and waiting for public or legislative opinion to catch up with them.

Presidential scholar Richard Neustadt has observed that the power to persuade is the primary instrument at the President's disposal as he attempts to move a program through a separately elected, co-equal branch of government. Presidents have used this tool both in their own relations with Members of Congress and through the "bully pulpit" (Theodore Roosevelt's pithy term for using public pressure to influence a reluctant Congress). In recent years, Presidents have increasingly relied on the White House Office of Legislative Liaison to keep them advised of sentiment on Capitol Hill and to coordinate their legislative strategies.

GETTING THE ADMINISTRATION ON TRACK FOR SUCCESS

To be successful on Capitol Hill with legislation that advances his policies, a President must weigh several factors. One of the most elementary is to make sure that Congress is clear about who speaks for the President.

Who Speaks for the President

Too often, Presidents devote insufficient attention to this task. As top Nixon and Ford aide Tom Korologos notes, President Kennedy had a shaky start with Congress because he did not make it clear that the Special Assistant to the President for Congressional Relations Larry O'Brien was his spokesman. Indeed, three or four months into the Kennedy Administration, Speaker of the House Sam Rayburn commented

Tom Korologos

to Bryce Harlow, O'Brien's predecessor in the Eisenhower Admin-istration, that he did not know who had taken Harlow's place. In effect, Harlow let O'Brien know that he was an invisible man, as far as the Speaker was concerned.

Kennedy swiftly corrected the matter by emphasizing O'Brien's role at his next meeting with the congressional leadership. As Korologos recalls:

> [The President] interrupted [comments being made by O'Brien], and he said, "Oh, by the way, gentle-men and ladies, I want you to know that Larry O'Brien is our congressional affairs person. When Larry speaks, I speak. He is my voice and eyes and ears. Go ahead, Larry." From that day forward, we all came to know the legendary job that Larry did. ... So the President needs to make clear to the lead-ers at the outset which of his aides he trusts to nego-tiate on his behalf. They need to know who can speak for him. They must know that the congres-sional relations person can get to the President immediately and turn back an issue on which they're working.

Gary Andres, who was President Bush's deputy in the legisla-tive affairs team, adds that it is just as important that Congress know who does *not* speak for the President. As Martin Anderson, Reagan's chief domestic policy adviser, and others have noted, many Presidents allow their administrations to lose momentum on Capitol Hill by permitting Cabinet secretaries to freelance (See Chapter 4). Presidents must make sure that it is clear which White House and agency staff are authorized to speak with the Hill. According to Andres:

> [I]t's important for any White House that's working with Congress to ... have a staff of people that are designated, and kind of anointed, by the President to be his congressional affairs people. The one thing you'll learn if you ever work in a congressional affairs office, in an administration, or in a White House is that everybody wants to do congressional affairs, and not everybody *should* do congressional affairs. It's important for the President and the Chief of Staff to have an enforcement mechanism in place where his people who are designated to work with Congress are the people who work with Congress, that there are swift and firm sanctions for anyone else who's not supposed to deal with Congress who gets involved in that job.

When Pat Griffin was Director of Legislative Affairs for the Clinton Administration, he also recognized the need to keep staff on a tight rein. But, he says, it became more and more difficult as the term wore on and the Democrats lost the House:

I met with the legislative affairs folks of each of the major departments, and even the sub-Cabinet-level agencies. In the first year that I was there…we didn't have a problem about people getting out ahead of us. What they wanted to do was to bring the White House into some of their issues. What I was doing at that point was managing the issues out of the White House. Given that we had so many, we were trying to prioritize. We were trying to use the agencies to work their people on the Hill for us. However, that changed when we lost control in the Congress. Then we brought all the issues into the White House and were concerned about being able to manage the message, because our fear was that our Cabinet folks would get too cozy with the chairmen of the other party in order to work their agenda and might compromise a larger strategy. So the dynamic changed dramatically.

Getting the Little Things Right

Senior White House aides and the designated legislative staff can veer badly off track if they forget Washington's mores and customs. Jimmy Carter's White House learned early that little mistakes by those new to Washington can be costly, as Korologos recalls:

At the inauguration, when Tip O'Neill, who was Speaker of the House at the time, asked for a couple extra tickets to the inauguration, Hamilton Jordan wouldn't give them to him. From that point on, Mr. O'Neill used to refer to Hamilton, the Chief of Staff, as "Hannibal Jerkin." The little things kill you in this business. As Max Friedersdorf, my colleague in the Nixon years, used to say, the most important thing is to know what kind of cigars Tip O'Neill smokes and where you seat Mrs. [John] McClellan, the Chairman of the [Senate] Appropriations Committee's wife, at the next dinner.

It is also important to remember that the administration's staff exists, in part, to respond to requests for information. And it must keep track of an immense amount of legislation. If the administration is not properly staffed to provide information and track legislation in ways that are satisfactory to members of both parties, problems are sure to follow. As Korologos explains:

[C]onsider the myriad issues that face an executive branch in its dealing with 535 members of Congress; 25,000 or 30,000, however many it is now, staffers up there; 10,000 bills introduced every couple years; more than 250 committees and subcommittees poking and jabbing at every piece of legislation there is. I haven't even touched on the thousands of phone calls that are generated every day. A couple of numbers to make the point: I've read in the paper recently, the Pentagon alone receives more than 100,000 written congressional inquiries a year. That's an average of 200 per Congressman. On every working day, the Pentagon receives 2,500 phone calls from Capitol Hill. Lord only knows how many reports and hearing preparations they're required.

According to Andres, mistakes are often made, particularly by junior staff, because incoming administrations often lack any real orientation program:

> [E]ven though it seems obvious that a lot of people who come into the job to work with Congress in moving an agenda have a lot of experience in that area, there really isn't a very good orientation mechanism involved for new people coming into an administration, or coming into a White House, to know what kind of job to do. ... I started on day one for President Bush. We walked into the White House. Were it not for some of the old Reagan Administration holdovers who were still using the phones and helping, we wouldn't know where the bathrooms were.

> So I think programs like [Heritage's Mandate for Leadership series] that try to put together some help to future administrations, whether they be Republicans or Democrats, in terms of how to do their job better, and how the White House can work better with Congress, are very valuable and very needed from my perspective.

ACHIEVING SUCCESS ON CAPITOL HILL

To be generally successful on Capitol Hill, the President must use his teams to develop a relationship with the power brokers of both parties. This is usually no easy matter, points out American University Professor James Thurber, a scholar of American government. First, seats in Congress are generally safe, meaning that a President can use political pressure only to a limited degree. Moreover, despite the increase of partisanship in recent years, congressional leaders still find it difficult to keep their members in line:

> There are 36 seats or so that are competitive within a margin of error right now in the House of Representatives .... The electoral setting in this bicameral setting is that we have weak control of recruitment by political parties. We have individualism .... That's a

major factor. The way people run for political office, how negative the campaigns are, what they do to win, and where they receive their primary financial support has an impact on their behavior after they get into office.

The Problems of a Divided Government

Thurber notes that this individualism reinforces the challenge that divided government has presented to most administrations:

> From 1887 to 1952, there were only eight years when we had divided party government, 12 percent of the time. From 1952 to 2000, we've had divided party government 75 percent of the time. When you have weak parties not controlling recruitment and not having a great deal of discipline over Members in the House of Representatives and Senate, that itself have their money coming from independent sources, specialized interests, combined with divided party government, it's surprising anything can get done.

Thurber adds that the President's difficulties in working with Congress are exacerbated by a lack of comity on the Hill that has resulted from bitter campaigns and partisanship within Congress. For example, Thurber notes, Speaker of the House Newt Gingrich and Minority Leader Richard Gephardt did not meet alone for Gingrich's duration as Speaker, instead talking to each other only in groups or by press conference:

> This is an example of the lack of comity, which makes it very difficult to govern on the Hill. The relationship between the President and the Congress is difficult. We also have, as part of the political environment that Pat [Griffin] mentioned, what I would call hyper-pluralism...extreme pluralism that is reinforced by strategic contributions by specialized interests. There's nothing wrong with pluralism. We have it under our First Amendment rights. Groups have a right to express themselves with money. But I think that it makes it very difficult for the President to build a coalition on the Hill, although he can break through it.

Working with the President's Party

Faced with this lack of comity, the President must take great care in the way he works with his own party in Congress, especially when his party is in the minority. As Gary Andres learned:

> We had a Democratic Congress and a Republican White House ....We were always facing trade-offs. You tried to negotiate with the Democrats and pass

laws. Or you tried to build your party and work with your party in Congress. The Republicans were always mad at us. Sometimes we were working too closely with the Democrats. The Democrats got mad at us if we worked too closely with the Republicans. So there's a whole series of trade-offs there that the next administration is going to have to face. It's really important to recognize that.

It is also important for the President to make sure that his own party in Congress understands his policy and political goals. As Griffin cautions:

I think one of the toughest things that a President has to do, of either party, is to help explain to members of his own party where his interests are not exactly the same as his party's congressional interests. That's a tough conversation, let me tell you. It goes a lot better when you're higher in the polls. ... It doesn't go well at all when you're not.... [I]f you've "gone native" and you're making too many of the sympathetic arguments why the President can't take on the congressional interests of his party, that's a kiss of death inside.

But that tension is an important one. [It's important to get it] on the table sooner, rather than later. Make it clear, that's what [I] may need to do at times, but also when you can count on me being solid. We didn't do a very good job of that. I think there was a lot of uneasiness with us, no matter what we were doing.

Building the Right Relationships

Equally important to Reagan's success, says *Washington Times* political correspondent Donald Lambro, was the trust and even friendship he developed among his political adversaries:

He kept the lines of communication open. I was reminded of this the other day watching "The American Experience" documentary on Reagan. It showed Tip O'Neill on the phone after he had been defeated, talking to the President, giving him the vote and saying, "Well, old pal, you've won. Wish you the best of luck."

They had a relationship that did develop. They talked after 6:00 p.m., when they could get together and put the partisan war away. O'Neill would go over there. They would have a drink, Reagan and O'Neill, finally willing to compromise at the end of the process.

Thanks to these relationships, says Lambro, Reagan was able to reach the kind of successful compromises on key issues that have eluded Clinton but could await the next President:

> Reagan, for all of his combativeness and principle, in the end always was willing to compromise to get what he could. I think when the history of Clinton is written, it will be this incredible political hostility that I think marked his presidency towards the other party on the Hill. You're not going to get anything done with that kind of approach....
>
> [O]n the lines of communications for Reagan, when you think back now, it was really extraordinary. Go back to the budget fights. We're not talking about just lines of communication. The Reagan White House had Democrats in the Democratic caucuses coming out and calling the White House. ... They were working hand in glove with what we call the "Blue Dog Democrats" now. So you had about 60 Democrats, but they were working hand in glove on getting their tax plan through, getting their budget through. Then, after the 1984 landslide, the big thing that Reagan won, of course, was the tax reform, which he ran on. Two people that they eventually worked very closely on were named Bradley and Gephardt. People forget, because Bradley and Gephardt now are so partisan, but back then, they had a bill. Their big shtick was to broaden the tax base and lower the rate. That's what Ronald Reagan wanted to do. You had the 1986 tax bill that he got through, that he got a lot of credit for, but was very much based on the Bradley–Gephardt tax plan.
>
> I think that's the parallel for the next presidency. You have the Breaux–Lieberman Medicare reform bill. They're people a Republican could work with. [Patrick] Moynihan and Bob Kerrey want to let you put two percent of your payroll taxes into stocks and mutual funds and bonds. They'll be gone, but there are Democrats who support their plan.

This does not ignore the good old-fashioned largesse that is usually necessary to cement a compromise or to give the President the final few votes he needs in a close call. Reagan was quite willing to dole out taxpayer money to win the larger budget battle, recalls Lambro:

> I remember sitting in a room with David Stockman after one big fight, and he told me, "You wouldn't believe how much money we had to spend for the buy-offs," as he called them, for the giveaways, to get certain Democratic votes.

But giveaways may end up being the price for insufficient attention to other aspects of winning support. As Pat Griffin says of the NAFTA [North American Free Trade Agreement] vote during the Clinton Administration:

> I don't think we made the case effectively across the country. We won it by opening up the candy store with highway spurs and trips on Air Force One and State Department dinners. That's how we put that over the top. It wasn't really strategy.

Taking, and Keeping, the Initiative

The President and his staff should realize that political capital is on the line on key votes. Picking these fights carefully, and winning them, is crucial to the perceived power of the administration. As an example, Tom Korologos points to an early Reagan effort to win congressional approval to sell surveillance aircraft to Saudi Arabia:

> President Reagan became President [and] two or three months later they had a big fight on AWACS.... [All] of a sudden the White House is up to its ears in passing an AWACS program. It passed. You never heard another word about it. Had they lost that, the stories out on the street would have been, this is a weak presidency, that they can't even pass a big deal like their AWACS thing, which they had expended so much capital on, and now they suffer the political consequences.

Even with one or both Houses of Congress in the hands of the other party, a President can control the initiative, as both Reagan and Clinton ably demonstrated. According to American University's James Thurber, a President is most likely to be able to build a coalition for a policy if he focuses on certain key tactical requirements:

> Very basically, if the President can clearly define a problem, or what the threat is, and go to the American public, usually above the heads of Congress, and then state a clear solution or mission that's very simple, and he has strong interest groups behind that particular mission, there's the perception, if not the reality, that there's no limit on resources with respect to the particular mission and problem. Finally, there [must be] a central core of authority driving that mission to solve the problem. If you have those, if you have that situation politically, you get things passed.

Thurber argues that Desert Storm was a good example of putting these elements in place, leading to a great Capitol Hill success for President Bush:

It was a clear definition of the problem, a clear statement of the mission. "This will not stand." Everybody understood what that meant. He went to the international community, built a coalition, then went to the Hill, had a debate with strong interest groups behind his mission, weak interest groups opposing it.

On the other hand, President Clinton's sweeping health care proposal collapsed because the needed elements were not in place. There was no public consensus on the problem, and the proffered solution involved a mission statement that was 1,585 complex pages in length. Moreover, says Thurber:

It went to 24 committees and subcommittees on Capitol Hill, in a highly decentralized structure. It was bound to fail. You had strong interest groups all over the place fighting each other, saying, "Yes, I'm for reform, but over there, not here."

THE IMPORTANCE OF A FOCUSED AGENDA

It is important, of course, for the President to remember that he is not the only one with an agenda. To be successful, he will have to have a give-and-take with the congressional leadership. The balance of those compromises will depend to a significant extent on the degree to which the President has articulated a clear legislative agenda. While Reagan's agenda was clear, Bush's was not, and that weakened his position. Explains Bush's aide Gary Andres:

When President Bush was first elected, there was a very famous comment that was quoted in a lot of newspapers when John Sununu, the Chief of Staff, was asked, "What do you want from Congress?" He said, "Well, we don't really want Congress to do anything." It was a well-intentioned comment, because I think he thought, well, with a Democratic Congress, what is a Republican President going to really get from them? But it kind of came out all wrong, so we want to remind people that it's good to have an agenda.

That agenda, says *National Journal* political correspondent Richard Cohen, will be most potent on Capitol Hill if the President emphasizes and reiterates it throughout his campaign.

Going back at least to Kennedy, and maybe all the way back to Roosevelt ... Presidents who have been able to do the most after they were elected were those who ran with a strong message during a campaign. I think, again, going back to Roosevelt, the two best examples of Presidents who ran with a campaign agenda were Ronald Reagan in 1980, obviously with a tax cut, and to some extent spending cuts. Lyndon Johnson in 1964, ran on the Great Society, not only Medicare, anti-poverty programs, civil rights, and other issues.

In each case, there was a strong message. In each case, for various reasons, the President was elected overwhelmingly. In each case, the President succeeded in Congress even though, in Reagan's case, he had to deal with a Democratic, at least an ostensibly Democratic, majority in the House. ... [R]ecent history shows that it's very difficult to lead legislatively on an issue that hasn't been discussed during the campaign.

Furthermore, if a President has raised an issue during his campaign, he may be able to sidestep Congress and fan public pressure on Capitol Hill. While Clinton has managed to do this to thwart many congressional measures, Donald Lambro points to Reagan as the model for bringing all the elements together, including public opinion, to achieve his own agenda:

All these things that have been said here today remind me, once again, to go back to the Reagan model, which I think is going to be the governing model for future Presidents. It was very simple. He laid down his markers very early. He applied public pressure on the Congress so that he could negotiate from strength. I think no one would disagree that he had a tremendous talent for applying public pressure and getting the letters and cards coming in, the phone calls, in to Congress.

PARTICIPANTS

Running the Largest Corporation in the World
April 18, 2000
St. Regis Hotel
Washington, D.C.

THE HONORABLE EDWIN MEESE III
Former Counsellor, President Ronald Reagan

Presenters

JAMES BURNLEY
Former Secretary of Transportation for President Ronald Reagan

GERALD CARMEN
Former Administrator of the General Services Administration for President Ronald Reagan

DONALD DEVINE
Director of the Office of Personnel Management for President Ronald Reagan

STEVEN KELMAN
Administrator of the Office of Federal Procurement (OMB) for President Bill Clinton

CHARLES KOLB
Former Deputy Assistant to President George Bush for Domestic Policy

GEORGE NESTERCZUK
Former Staff Director of the House Subcommittee on Civil Service

JOSEPH WRIGHT
Former Director of the Office of Management and Budget for President Ronald Reagan

Commentators

PAUL LIGHT
Vice President and Government Studies Director, The Brookings Institution

ROBERT MARANTO
Professor, Villanova University

CHAPTER VII:
MANAGING THE
LARGEST CORPORATION
IN THE WORLD

"Just as every President comes in with an agenda with some vision for the world order, some vision for social policy, economic policy, tax policy, you need to devote some attention to the management side of the picture."

—George Nesterczuk

A critical factor in the success of any President is his ability to ensure that the rest of the executive branch faithfully executes the law and carries out his administrative directives. Yet managerial duties remain one of the least interesting aspects of the President's job, not just to the media and the public but, all too often, to the President himself.

To be sure, whenever a crisis develops or a disaster occurs within the executive branch, and media and congressional attention is focused on the particular agency affected, there may be a flurry of corrective action. Otherwise, however, the work that anonymous civil servants perform is rarely given serious attention by the President, whether that work facilitates or impedes his agenda.

As the head of the executive branch, the President presides over an extensive enterprise of agencies that perform vital functions and often have overlapping jurisdictions. The scale of the management challenge is staggering: The federal government would be equivalent to a corporation with almost $2 trillion in annual revenues and a workforce of over 4 million.

In a tongue-in-cheek memo to his budget director, Franklin D. Roosevelt expressed how difficult it is for a President to take hold of the government he supposedly leads:

I agree with the Secretary of the Interior. Please have it carried out so that fur-bearing animals remain in the Department of the Interior.

You might find out if any Alaska bears are still supervised by a) War Department, b) Department of Agriculture, c) Department of Commerce. They have all had jurisdiction over Alaska bears in the past and many embarrassing situations have been created by the mating of a bear belonging to one Department with a bear belonging to another Department.

P.S. I don't think the Navy is involved, but it may be. Check the Coast Guard. You never can tell.

In a more serious vein, Dwight D. Eisenhower unleashed his famous temper at an army general who gloated at the failure of the Navy's Vanguard missile. One goal he never realized was ending inter-service rivalries by merging several branches into one.

The frustrations experienced by Roosevelt and Eisenhower occurred when the federal government was but a shadow of what it has become. Today, the United States government employs millions of people; oversees a vast empire of buildings, property, and land; funds and conducts research; issues millions of dollars worth of contracts; and is a major purchaser of goods and services. It also maintains a large defense enterprise, making it responsible for the well-being of its armed forces and the acquisition and upkeep of state-of-the-art weaponry.

The President's job entails seeing that these enterprises are performed in the most professional manner possible. Poor administration and oversight can slow the nation's competitive edge and endanger its security. Incompetence or corruption can erode the public confidence in an administration.

As Presidents discharge the managerial aspects of the presidency, they must strike a balance between career civil servants, who have professional training and the institutional memory necessary to perform tasks assigned them, and the political appointees who oversee them. As a result, Presidents must make maximum use of the power of persuasion as well as incentives that encourage mutual cooperation and loyalty. They must also bring management tools and practices that have proven to be effective in the private sector to the government.

This may be exceptionally difficult. Vested interests have a stake in the status quo, and opponents of change can make their voice heard at congressional inquiries and in the media. Nevertheless, Presidents have at their command tools they can use to make a well-managed bureaucracy enact parts of their agenda. The most important of these tools is the President's ability to motivate the staff at all levels of his administration.

THE CHIEF EXECUTIVE

The complexities of management are rarely of great interest to politicians, whose primary passion is usually policy. Even Jimmy Carter, the President probably most interested in the science of government, confessed that he found the minutiae of civil service reform boring. Yet, George Nesterczuk, who served in Ronald Reagan's Office of Personnel Management as well as in Cabinet departments, declares that it is essential for the President to appreciate the importance of his commitment to a management agenda. Failure to do so, Nesterczuk says, will make it difficult for the President to mobilize the government around his policies:

James Burnley, Charles Kolb, and Gerald Carmen

> Holding [political leaders] accountable is the natural way of managing government. You do not need to micromanage those people. If you've entrusted them with your agenda, if you keep them in the loop through Cabinet meetings, through senior-level staff meetings, then you don't need to manage the agenda. If you go off track, you always have the option of letting them go and replacing them with someone else. Unlike a career civil servant who is there long after you're gone, political leadership can be changed. That's really the way we do manage a political agenda: that ultimate accountability of replacement, losing the job.

> The extent to which that kind of flexibility could be extended into the federal workforce will depend on a President's management agenda. Just as every President comes in with an agenda with some vision for the world order, some vision for social policy, economic policy, tax policy, you need to devote some attention to the management side of the picture.

In order to appreciate the President's proper role as head of government, it is useful to distinguish between two broad approaches that have been taken by most occupants of the Oval Office. Charles Kolb, who served in both the Reagan and Bush

119

Administrations, believes that Presidents can be divided into two broad types: conviction or managerial leaders. This distinction, Kolb believes, predicts the degree of success Presidents have in achieving their agenda:

> I have a bias that the most successful Presidents, at least in the 20th century, have tended to be "conviction Presidents," as opposed to what I call "managerial Presidents." It doesn't mean that all managerial Presidents are failures; but conviction Presidents, I think, tend to have a longer impact on the affairs of the country. As conviction Presidents, I would rate [Franklin] Roosevelt, [Harry] Truman, Lyndon Johnson, Ronald Reagan. As managerial Presidents, [Dwight] Eisenhower, [John F.] Kennedy, [Richard] Nixon, [Gerald] Ford, [Jimmy] Carter, [George] Bush, and [Bill] Clinton.

Still, adds Kolb, a conviction President will not necessarily achieve the restructuring of the government that he may want:

> Let me give you an example. Ronald Reagan, I think, was an outstanding conviction President, but many of you will remember when Ronald Reagan came to town, he wanted to abolish the Department of Education, crusaded with vigilance to eliminate the Department of Education.
>
> When Ronald Reagan came to Washington, there were 150 separate federal education programs. The first couple of years there was a block grant that consolidated a number of those programs, it went from 150 down to 120. When Ronald Reagan left Washington and George Bush became President, how many federal education programs were there? Anybody remember? 208.

Kolb maintains that such failures occur because new administrations inherit a governmental structure that does not focus on the new President's agenda. This does not mean that civil servants are bad people, Kolb emphasizes, but that they simply have no particular commitment to the new President's perspective on government.

As a result, says Robert Maranto, who taught at the Federal Executive Institute, the President must understand something basic: He is not the top manager or classic CEO of a corporation; but he is a leader:

> The President is not a manager. One manages an office. One does not manage the 2 million-person executive branch of government. It's a big elephant. You try to push it and pull it. You don't really manage it. I think what a President can do is set the conditions for good management....

Instead of managing, what the President does, one hopes, is lead. Presidential leadership skills are very different from management skills. A great President—and I think all the previous speakers have mentioned this in one way or another—knows his goals, sells those goals to the administration and to the American people, and selects people who can implement those goals. A President does not get down in the weeds to figure out exactly how his goals are being implemented.

In contrast, a manager is someone who can adapt and adopt someone else's vision and implement that vision. A good government manager is patriotic, hard-working, honest, and politically astute but has to be flexible enough to implement either Democratic or Republican visions of the national interest.

This perspective, adds Maranto, explains why a President like Ronald Reagan was relatively successful in running the government:

Ronald Reagan, in my view, would have made a very poor government manager.

He was very inattentive to detail, arguably even occasionally lazy. Because Reagan had strong convictions, it's impossible for me to imagine him implementing, say, Jimmy Carter's fiscal policy or Richard Nixon's foreign policy. He just couldn't have done it.

Reagan would have made a very poor career government manager, but he was, I think, a pretty good President. He knew what he wanted to do. He was able to persuade both his own Administration and the American people that it was the right thing to do. He was good at picking people to implement his vision.

LEADING THE CIVIL SERVICE

The President's senior officials must echo his leadership and dedication in order for a sense of commitment to permeate the government. Don Devine directed the Office of Personnel Management under Ronald Reagan and is Professor of Government and Politics at the University of Maryland. Like others in the Reagan Administration, Devine argues that the universal sense of commitment was a key element in the success of the Administration in motivating a skeptical civil service. Former Attorney General Edwin Meese notes that the top White House staff and the President urged senior agency appointees to make every effort to impart Reagan's mission to their civil servants (see Chapter 3).

Dr. Robert Moffit of The Heritage Foundtion questioning Don Devine.

Both Meese and Devine, however, concede that in many administrations—even in the Reagan Administration—this charge was not always achieved, in part because there are always appointees who do not see the enactment of the President's program as their highest priority. As Devine explains:

A very large percentage, even in the Reagan Administration, did not have [Reagan's program] as their first priority. As someone said in a later administration, comparing it to Reagan, "What do you think about Reagan's recruiting people on a basis of ideology?" This personnel officer said, "We don't believe in ideology in this administration. We believe in resumes."

Describing his experience in the Bush Administration, Charles Kolb explains that simple everyday concerns can weaken the determination of presidential appointees:

Let me give you the exact statement that was said by one senior person in that administration: "Our people don't have agendas. They have mortgages. They want jobs." I submit to you there is a fundamental difference in perspective if your first goal is paying your mortgage as opposed to figuring out how to implement an agenda.

Kolb points out, however, that if appointees do have a sense of purpose and are willing to deal with the civil service in a straightforward and sensible way, they can gain the support of their permanent staff:

[Education Secretary William] Bennett wanted to reduce the number of regulations that the Education Department was issuing, so he put in place a task force basically to try and deregulate the department. I remember working on that task force.

One of the things we tried to do was to get the bureaucracy to examine itself—not an easy thing. We had people from 20 different offices around the department get together. I remember proposing to them one day that we go through an exercise which I literally called "dumb things that we do." This was by and large with the career bureaucracy.

They looked at me like I was crazy. You want us to do what? Examine what we currently do in terms of issuing proposed rules and other things and come back in two weeks with an example of a dumb thing that we do? Do you want me to lose my job? I went first with some stupid things we did in the General Counsel's Office. That kind of raised the comfort level.

Throughout the course of the next year, people got into this. They realized I wasn't trying to get them to report on themselves. I wasn't trying to get them to lose their jobs. I was trying to get them to be more efficient in dealing with their customers, the people they regulated or the people they shouldn't be regulating. So if you can do something like that, you can get a sense of self-perspective, step back, take a look at what you're doing.

Gerald Carmen, who was Administrator of the General Services Administration (GSA) in the first Reagan term, adds that when appointees work with the civil service, it is critically important that they not give in to the hysteria with which the bureaucracy will respond to change:

I met with about 50 of the key executives in GSA around a huge table to discuss what we were going to do [about budget cuts]. If you had heard the moaning and groaning around that room from every department head, from every commission head, from everybody's head. It was unbelievable.

They went around the room, and they explained how people would be in the streets. People would be out of work. Press would be bad. It was a total disaster for some 30,000 people.

I kept looking at the budget in front of me, and it had millions of dollars of training. It had millions of dollars in travel. It had millions of dollars in this. It had millions of dollars in that. None of which I probably understood, but I understood a dollar sign. Finally, they came back to me. I said, "Look, fellows and gals, we're keeping both those cuts. I'm not putting anybody on the street. You are. You've got a budget that includes a lot of things besides people. If you can handle it the way you should, people would be working for us at the end of September. If you can't, it's your fault, not mine." Come the middle of budget year, we had a surplus. Nobody was on the street. Everything ran like clockwork. ...

These obstacles that we faced in government that are thrown up by those who actually know how to run government versus those of us that didn't, aren't

> real. If you know what the President wants, and if you get advice from the White House as we had from Ed Meese or from Joe Wright and the others that were there, you can get this job done.

Robert Maranto notes that while cooperation with the civil service makes eminent sense, political appointees must assess who will be cooperative and uncooperative, and plan accordingly:

> For the appointees themselves, I would urge them to conduct reconnaissance of their new agencies by asking all the previous appointees they can find of either party, of any administration, which career bureaucrats they can work with and which ones they have to watch. More often than not, political appointees, even of different parties, will agree on which career executives are effective, which are ineffective, and which are speed bumps, and you deal with all of those.

THE NATURE OF THE FEDERAL BUREAUCRACY

Although many Americans think generally of the federal government as a huge corporation, in reality it functions profoundly differently than do private institutions. It poses an enormous challenge to a President attempting to move the government in a particular direction.

Maranto explains that there are several key differences that a President must confront. For example, long-term planning is difficult, if not impossible, in government. Severe limits exist on the ability of government managers to redeploy resources and people and to hire the people they need to complete a job. Moreover, says Maranto:

> A government is a fish bowl. Imagine if in a private corporation your chief competitors served on your board of directors. That's really the situation in government. That's the situation that the founding fathers gave us, and it mostly works fairly well. But it is a great vexation to those in the executive branch of government. As one of my friends who's a career civil servant likes to put it, we have a bunch of micromanaging opportunists in Congress. It's true now. It's always been true. It will always be true.

> More than anything else, in business we know our goals and we know our measures of success. At least in the days before e-commerce, success was measured in terms of profits: Are you making money? How do we measure the goals of government organizations when we can't agree on what they should be doing?

In part because of the process by which Congress creates government programs, often with inadequate attention to programs already in existence, government agencies tend to be balkanized and uncoordinated. As a result, is it often difficult for the head of an agency to obtain the information needed to make good decisions. When Edwin Meese became Attorney General during the Reagan Administration, he took a number of steps to tackle this problem:

> One of the things that I found when I took over the Department of Justice is that you have a lot of duchies and fiefdoms. It's hard to get them to talk to each other.

> So I set up four boards that were crosscutting boards. One was a departmental resources board, which brought division heads for the first time into the budgeting process. I put my deputy as the chairman of that board. The Director of the FBI was on it and a couple of other people. Before that, budgets had been made by what I call the green eyeshade people, the accountants. Now, because you had management people deciding the budget for the department and making the recommendations to me, all of a sudden division heads started coming to those meetings. So you had a crosscurrent of information there from the people in charge.

> I set up a personnel policy board, which did the same thing and brought people discussing what the personnel policies would be so we'd have a common personnel policy throughout the department.

> A third board was our strategic planning board that was made up of the heads of all of our principal components so that they would be talking about where the department ought to be five years from now, which was one year after our administration would have left, but so that they would at least be working in that direction, be looking at e-commerce—e-commerce wasn't in the field then, but those kinds of future developments.

> The fourth one, which was an interesting one to me, was a research and development board. Government does a lot of research. Every department does. We had research happening in the FBI and the Bureau of Prisons, all over, including the agencies that were supposed to do research like the National Institute of Justice. Nobody had ever coordinated the research. This board's purpose was to coordinate research projects. The first thing they did was do an inventory of all the research projects. They found the department was doing, I think, 687 different

projects, many of them in the same field but without any coordination between them.

Obstacles to Good Management Practices

Nesterczuk warns that recent trends will complicate the federal government for its managers, especially if they are conservative-leaning. He believes entrepreneurialism fosters arbitrariness among government officials, and he questions the fairness of its recent applications. One trend that concerns Nesterczuk is the decentralization of control:

> In the past few years, the trend has been away from strong leadership control, much more to decentralization. Part of the National Performance Review agenda, the "reinventing government" agenda, was to create an entrepreneurial government. For me, that's a pretty scary notion, particularly in that the entrepreneurs were supposed to be the front-line federal employees who interface with the public.

> Conceptually, that's nice. That's certainly built on a private-sector model of trying to build profit centers as close to your customers as possible. Then you look at the bottom line to see whether or not they're delivering the goods.

> Unfortunately, in the government, we don't have those kinds of bottom-line measures of success of performance. As a result, you've got a prescription for letting a thousand flowers bloom. If you believe that one of the basic tenets of government is that everyone be treated equally, equitably, and fairly, you cannot do that through an entrepreneurial model, because at that point you have a thousand bureaucrats scattered from Montana to Maine to Florida interpreting the rules their own particular way.

Steven Kelman, Professor of Public Management at Harvard University's John F. Kennedy School of Government, argues the opposite, based on his studies of government organization and his service with President Clinton's Office of Federal Procurement:

> I think it's a recipe for disaster [in terms of] the performance of the government to chain the government to the kinds of bureaucratic rule-boundedness that's being abandoned in droves in the private sector and that also leads to many problems with the government.

Another recent trend that Nesterczuk notes is the increased limits placed on the power of managers:

The next administration's going to be inheriting a whole new set of partners. There was an Executive Order in place that created a National Partnership Council, which is a new way of managing government with your friendly local labor union.

That may work for the Clinton Administration. I don't fault them for taking that approach to getting their job done. They have natural political allies in the labor unions, federal employee unions. If those allies permit them to shortcircuit their management structure to hold their management structure accountable to a political agenda, that's fine. That's a very efficient way of getting the job done.

If, however, that partner is on a different ideological agenda than you are, you have a major problem. At that point, you have gridlock in government and not progress. That's the potential danger for a new administration coming in inheriting these partnership councils. That's one of the reasons I believe that a more conservatively oriented administration in the future would have a much more difficult job in getting its agenda in place.

Another trend, says Nesterczuk, is placing limitations on a manager's ability to rate employees:

If you're going to downsize your organization, you ought to be able to keep your best people first and separate your worst performers. With a pass-fail system, which is what we've been going to, in effect you have no measure of performance to add to your retention consideration, because the passes are all passes. There's no distinction between your best performers and your moderate performers. The fails get special protection anyway. They have due process, so they can't be removed until due process is completed.

A more significant problem for performance and morale, says Maranto, is the host of restrictions placed on firing employees:

Right now, my former employer, the U.S. Office of Personnel Management, estimates that there are about 65,000 non-performing personnel in government, people who do little or no work and are occasionally dangerous to their coworkers and you can't get rid of them. Or at least it's very, very difficult to get rid of them. In a given year, we fire about 150 people for cause and about another 1,500 people for breaking the law.

So there's about 65,000 people who we should fire but only a small number we do fire. That's not a huge number of people. It's fewer than 5 percent of federal employees. Most federal employees do a fairly good job, but that 5 percent has a very pernicious impact on the civil service in a bunch of ways.

In part, it hurts morale because they get the same pay raises as the rest of us while we have to do their work. But in part, it saps the legitimacy of the civil service. Most Americans do not have tenure. I think it's no accident that college professors and school teachers, public school teachers, have all come under attack, because most Americans cannot understand why they don't have tenure and the public servants do. I think that's a very reasonable point.

A general problem with the federal government, Charles Kolb notes, is the way in which Congress, interest groups, and members of the civil service work together to support or oppose a President's agenda. This "iron triangle," Kolb says, was the impediment that rendered Reagan unable to eliminate or even scale back the Department of Education:

The example of Ronald Reagan and education illustrates another structure that I think is an impediment to a conviction President being able to manage. That is the interlocking structure, the relationship between the Congress, the bureaucracy, and the interest groups. It's trite to refer to it as the iron triangle, but it really does exist.

IMPROVING PERFORMANCE

Joseph Wright, who served as Director of the Office of Management and Budget during Ronald Reagan's presidency, warns that it is difficult for a President to improve the management of the federal government. Wright notes that history is littered with short-lived attempts to introduce management improvements:

Every four years, around six months before the presidential election, transition teams begin developing policy and personnel position papers for their incoming White House victors. Seldom do their efforts include recommendations on how to "manage" the vast enterprise that they plan to inherit. The President normally focuses on that later in his first year in office.

Almost every recent President eventually initiated numerous efforts to improve the management of the federal government once they realized that improvement was badly needed. But few of these efforts have survived the particular administration during which the initiative was announced. For example, President Johnson introduced a "war on waste" and the PPBS (Planning, Programming, Budgeting System) program throughout the executive branch, which was not continued under President Nixon.

President Nixon introduced FAR (Federal Assistance Review), which established departmental geographic regions, regional councils, and simplification of procurements and grants. The President also issued Circular A–44, which initiated a government-wide management improvement program. Under this program, OMB "Swat teams" held meetings with departments and agencies to set up goals for management improvement and to monitor the progress in achieving these goals. Finally, in 1974, the President established a government-wide MBO (Management by Objectives) system and announced it in his budget message. Most of these ambitious efforts established by President Nixon did not survive his Administration.

President Ford in 1976 initiated the PMI (President Management Initiatives) [program] to identify management improvement efforts, integrate these efforts into the budget process, and monitor the results. The PMI program was discontinued when President Carter was elected.

President Carter issued Circular A–117 (management improvement and the use of evaluation in the executive branch), where departments and agencies were asked to make management improvements following the best practices of both government and business and this effort was combined with zero-based budgeting. This effort was discontinued when President Reagan was elected.

President Reagan set up management reviews as part of the budget review process with the agencies. He also strengthened the President's Council on Integrity and Efficiency (PCIE), made up of the inspectors general in the agencies, to identify management improvements in support of their efforts to reduce waste, fraud, and abuse. He also issued a management report with each annual budget; installed the first government-wide chief financial officer; initiated standardization and consolidation of government-wide financial accounting, payroll, and personnel systems; installed the first government-wide ATM and lockbox system for cash management; began the use of credit cards for government employee expenses and purchases; and worked with Congress to improve credit management and controls. He called this ambitious effort "Reform 88," but as in the past, many of his initiatives were discontinued, even the mandated management report to the Congress.

Early in 1989, President Bush established a Presidential Management By Objective (MBO) program where each major agency identified key policy priorities which were to be monitored by OMB and those priorities were listed in his FY '91 Budget. This initiative was discontinued two years later.

Then, in 1993, President Clinton and Vice President Al Gore established the National Performance Review (NPR) that recommended 1,200 actions geared toward improving government services through technology. It is still underway and may or may not be continued.

Wright says that future Presidents should not think such initiatives are "boring," as Jimmy Carter once described them. They should not allow the efforts to lose steam because they are vitally important to keeping the bureaucracy in line with the will of the President and Congress. Moreover, Wright adds, Congress has been slowly giving the executive branch increased powers and obligations that the President can use to ensure that the agencies and civil service comply:

In 1982, Congress passed, at the request of the White House, the Prompt Payment Act requiring federal agencies to pay bills on time; the Debt Collection Act providing OMB with new authority to improve federal debt/credit management; the Federal Managers Financial Integrity Act, which gave OMB responsibility to oversee annual reviews of agency accounting administration control systems; and the Deficit Reduction Act of 1984, which required the President to submit an annual report as part of the budget which described the status of management improvement and cost-reduction initiatives in the federal government. The first report, entitled *Management of the United States Government*, was sent up with the FY 1986 budget.

Later, the Congress passed the Government Performance and Results Act of 1993 requiring federal departments and agencies to identify, track, and report on strategic plans to improve programs, along with implementation actions and costs or savings. This legislation goes further in requiring that OMB and the departments and agencies identify and measure their goals and the implementation of those goals. It links strategic plans to annual budgets and requires a formal reporting system.

Then, earlier this year, the House passed H.R. 2883, which requires federal agencies to submit "strategic plans" to achieve agency goals and requires inspectors general to audit their agencies' performance reports. More legislation along these lines, in my opinion, will be passed in the next few years.

Making Management a Priority

The next President, says Wright, has a real opportunity to make management improvement a cornerstone of his administration. Unless the President truly considers reform a priority, Wright warns, improvements will not occur, and a critical element in achieving a policy agenda will be lost. Wright also advises that a new President must understand that it takes a long time for reforms to be developed and instituted—and to cause change—which is why so many come to nothing. A resolution to improve management must be accompanied by a sense of urgency, Wright adds:

> It usually takes two years from the day that you start with a great idea to the time you get it appropriated to the time you can do a contract, to get it in place. It's normally going to be about three years. The next transition team is going to have to start right out of the box coming from the President. That new President is going to have to say, "This is important to me." It makes a difference. Give good examples … from a PR standpoint of why it makes a difference. It won't be boring then.

In addition, says Nesterczuk, a President may be able to convince Congress to go along with management reforms, but the President must take the lead if Capitol Hill is to implement needed reforms:

> The ultimate message here is for the next President: Congress will follow the lead. If you tell Congress that management is important, that personnel issues are important, that managing cash flows is important, Congress will respond. They view these kinds of issues as the prerogative of the executive branch. If the Chief Executive doesn't devote any attention to it, Congress won't either. So Congress is definitely not going to be the answer here. The President will be. He will need to set some kind of a management agenda.

Despite the challenges posed by the nature of the federal bureaucracy, a President today does have tools and powers at his disposal that will help him gain the active support of the civil service in pursuing his agenda. In addition, a President can introduce changes or advocate reforms in the law that will make his task easier.

Don Devine points out, for example, that President Carter put into place a more rigorous performance appraisal system with rewards and bonuses for superior performance and merit pay for high-level managers. This system encouraged civil servants to carry out the President's wishes. Unfortunately, these mechanisms gradually were eroded or lapsed. The next President, says Devine, should restore a system of appraisal.

In particular, says Charles Kolb, the administration should "try and find ways to change those personnel rules so that you can get rid of bad people and bring in good people." And, he notes, the administration should:

> look for ways to build accountability performance indicators—feedback loops, if you will—into your management process. This is one of the key areas where the federal government differs from the private sector.

Steven Kelman agrees that it is important for the President to make a strong case for incorporating better performance measurement and management systems:

> This should be seen not the way it's typically seen in this town, which is like a thermometer where you say, "This agency's doing X. Let's measure it, see how it does, and then either reward it, punish it, or whatever."

> That's part of it, but the more important part is that if you actually do this right and don't just develop a list of measures to send off to OMB but actually manage these measures the way a corporate executive would do, it's not just about a thermometer that goes in and tells you how you do. It's about improving the performance of the organization. Any organization that manages and takes performance measurements seriously is going to do better.

> But it won't happen without some pressure from the White House and from Congress. So if I had to give one priority in terms of a management agenda for the new administration, it would be performance measurement and performance management.

George Nesterczuk emphasizes the need to reform the compensation and benefits system, as well as to take a more sensible approach to staffing:

> We need to move to a market-based compensation system. Right now we have a one-size-fits-all pay system. That's close to dysfunctional in many occupations, and we're not attracting the right people, and we're not getting the best talent that we could as a result of that. There's no question we should be paying some people more. There is no question that

we're overpaying a huge part of that workforce. So we definitely need a more market-based compensation system.

Portable benefits. The retirement system is wonderful. It's very rich. It's very, very expensive. But in a workforce like we currently have, where people change jobs four or five times in their lifetimes, where they're not looking for a 30- to 40-year commitment with an employer, where they're looking to change careers, you need a benefit package that follows them around. Our benefit package with the government dates back to the 1930s and 1940s. So there's much that can be changed there to the benefit of the employees as well as the taxpayer. The unfunded liabilities in the retirement system are in the hundreds of billions of dollars. We're just basically putting off those responsibilities to future taxpayers.

Finally, a flexible staffing system. We're moving that way. One of the interesting fallouts from this takeover of government by federal unions has been that federal managers have fought back in a very clever way. If they cannot hold their workforce accountable, they let their workforce go. We've seen contracting out as we've never seen it before in this administration. That's one of the fundamental tenets of labor unions, to hold on to those jobs. What they're seeing by having asserted political control over a good sector of government is that those jobs are starting to slip between their fingers.

New technology, notes Kolb, also will be important to future administrations for a number of reasons:

The technology revolution is ultimately going to wash over the government and the nonprofit sector together. It has impacted the business community, which has gone through downsizing, rightsizing, reinventing. It also has impacted the military. If you look at the way the military is run now, it is a very different military than at the end of the Vietnam War.

The process is still underway with regard to government. Vice President Al Gore, I think, has done some good through the work that his aide Elaine Kamarck did. The next administration needs to continue that and drive it home further.

Finally, Don Devine, like Reagan's chief domestic policy assistant Martin Anderson, stresses the importance of Cabinet Councils (see Chapter 4). These councils bring a sense of direction to the top of the government pyramid, which can extend through the entire government apparatus. Devine recalls the importance of the Cabinet Councils to the Reagan Administration; they gave focus to the entire management team:

> One of the things that was enormously important in running our administration was the cabinet council, getting people focused on management issues at the very highest level, including many times meeting with the President on these issues. I saw it not so much from management itself, but giving strength and leadership and courage and vision to those who are out on the line doing the work.

PARTICIPANTS

The President and the Media
March 16, 2000
St. Regis Hotel
Washington, D.C.

THE HONORABLE EDWIN MEESE III
Former Counsellor, President Ronald Reagan

Presenters

MICHAEL DEAVER
Former Assistant to the President and Deputy Chief of Staff to President Ronald Reagan

BARRY TOIV
Former Deputy Press Secretary to President Bill Clinton

SANDER VANOCUR
Former NBC Television Correspondent

Commentators

TONY BLANKLEY
Former Press Secretary to the Speaker of the House Newt Gingrich

CARL CANNON
Government Executive Editor, National Journal

MARTHA KUMAR
Professor of Political Science, Towson University

ROBERT NOVAK
Syndicated Columnist

Selling the President's Program
April 6, 2000

Presenters

LYN NOFZIGER
Assistant to President Ronald Reagan for Political Affairs

LANDON PARVIN
Speechwriter to President Ronald Reagan

MICHAEL WALDMAN
Speechwriter to President Bill Clinton

Commentators

CAROL GELDERMAN
Professor of English, University of New Orleans

SICHAN SIV
Deputy Assistant to President George Bush for Public Liaison

KEN SMITH
Deputy Editor, Editorial Page, The Washington Times

KAREN TUMULTY
White House Correspondent, Time Magazine

ANNE WEXLER
Former Assistant to President Jimmy Carter for Public Liaison

CHAPTER VIII:
BUILDING PUBLIC SUPPORT FOR THE PRESIDENT'S AGENDA

"We always had a strategic plan. It began with the 100-day plan that we started through the transition under Ed Meese's supervision and ran through the first 100 days."
—Michael Deaver

No President can hope to enact an agenda—especially if it is an ambitious one—without public support. Public support can translate into votes in the legislature and cooperation within bureaucracies. But in order to obtain public support, Presidents have to devise ways to communicate effectively to the public through the prevailing media of their times and by the careful nurturing of key constituencies.

In the early days of the republic, James Madison's wife Dolley, a one-woman public relations operation, used her widely reported soirees as occasions to sell her husband's ideas to skeptics. George Washington, James Monroe, and Andrew Jackson endured the inconveniences of traveling by coach to different parts of the country to build support for their programs. They found they could reach more people this way, and regional papers that seldom saw a President were likely to print more of what they said.

Modern Presidents, of course, have also sought ways to reach the public over the heads of the Washington press establishment. The electronic age has assisted by bringing the President's voice and image into homes and by giving the President a larger and more visible role in the day-to-day life of the nation. Even the taciturn Calvin Coolidge took to the airwaves often enough to make his voice as recognizable to the public as those of popular entertainers. Franklin D. Roosevelt, through his "fireside chats," went a step further and created the impression that he was conversing with his audience rather than reading a formal address.

John F. Kennedy showed similar mastery over the new medium of television. Kennedy pioneered live, televised press conferences, and he adopted the use of direct broadcasts from the Oval Office, which his two predecessors had also given. Through these public contacts, Kennedy was able to move public opinion in his direction. The press conferences gave audiences a chance to see the President think in public, and reporters often functioned as his "straight men," conveying his latest witticism to the public.

Kennedy's skillful use of television altered the public's expectations of a President. People began to expect Presidents to be "great communicators." Of the Presidents who followed Kennedy, Ronald Reagan and Bill Clinton are usually thought to have been the most successful at meeting this relatively new requirement.

One of the challenges Presidents now face—even if their communication skills are good—is communicating their message to the public in an age of 24-hour news cycles, "investigative" and "advocacy" journalism through a multitude of media outlets. With numerous cable stations and the Internet, more and more people can tune out the President. Like entertainers, U.S. Presidents must fight for ratings and are no longer assured of airplay.

While technology affects the manner in which Presidents communicate, to be effective they still need to craft a strategy to reach the key groups that are necessary to build public support. And they need to create an effective team to coordinate this strategy.

From the nation's earliest days, Presidents have retained advisers to help them market their ideas and build support for their programs. George Washington began the practice by calling in junior advisers such as James Madison and Alexander Hamilton to assist him with his message and with addresses that he hoped would have a major impact.

Several Presidents had help in drafting speeches, addresses, and correspondence, but Warren Harding was the first to retain a staff member whose primary responsibility was ghostwriting. Franklin D. Roosevelt established a specific position within the White House for speechwriter Samuel Rosenman. Having a communications staff within the White House, and involving those writing speeches in the policy process, made it possible for writers to develop clear and consistent themes that conveyed the essence of the administration's policies. This pattern continued through several administrations, cresting with the synergistic relationship John F. Kennedy enjoyed with senior adviser and principal speechwriter Theodore C. Sorensen.

This model began to wane under Richard Nixon, who submerged speechwriting under the wider umbrella of outreach and communications, but it re-emerged somewhat under Ronald Reagan and Bill Clinton. Both understood how precise language could persuade others of the merits of their proposals.

Today, as Presidents reach out to special constituencies that comprise important elements of their political base, Presidents rely more and more on staff members who have standing with those that they hope to influence on the President's behalf. The White House has several offices—political affairs, intergovernmental affairs, and public liaison—that do this in different ways. While these offices all engage in two-

Michael Deaver, Barry Toiv, Sander Vanocur and Robert Novak

way dialogue, their principal purpose is to rally support behind the President's objectives. In order to perform their assigned roles, those who head these operations have to work in tandem with other parts of the White House organization, especially communications, press, and speechwriting. Since 1970, the speechwriting and press functions have been under the Office of White House Communications. Some of the panelists at the Heritage Mandate 2000 forums questioned the wisdom of that decision because it often has separated the speechwriting and press functions from policy development and implementation.

CREATING AN IMPRESSION WITH THE PUBLIC

Few Americans ever meet the President, or even his staff; therefore, the impression they have of the President depends almost completely on the images and words that reach them through the media. These impressions are conveyed through the technology available—from still photographs in FDR's day, to multiple television channels and the Internet in Clinton's. The impression a President conveys can affect the public's attitude toward his ideas. The experiences of recent Presidents indicate some of the critical elements of public relations to ensure that the American people form a favorable view of the new President and his policies.

Communicating a Clear and Coordinated Message

One of the master strategists of presidential communications, Ronald Reagan's Deputy Chief of Staff Michael Deaver, emphasizes the critical importance of having a clear and concise message—and of repeating it over and over again. As he puts it:

> What is important is knowing who you are and
> being comfortable with it, and understanding today
> that the camera doesn't lie; having a clear and con-

cise message, repeating it over and over again; and, finally, [having] the discipline to be able to keep everybody on that message.

Sometimes even the Great Communicator himself, Ronald Reagan, grew tired of constantly emphasizing one message during a trip. But Deaver recalls reminding Reagan of just how effective this could be—in this case the issue was education:

> I remember, after about a week and a half of this, being in Atlanta, flying back on Air Force One and the President throwing his speech cards across this table to me and saying "I'm not going to give the speech any more. This is ridiculous. I've been doing this for a week and a half now, and those guys"—meaning the media in the back of the plane—"aren't paying any attention to this."

> I said, "Well, Mr. President, let me just tell you that four days before you were in Atlanta, the local news there was covering the arrangements, talking to the local education people, talking to the mayor, the superintendent of education, watching and following the Secret Service and the advance people making the details. From the time this airplane set down in Atlanta until wheels up four hours later, you were live in one of the five major media markets in the country, and tomorrow the Secretary of Education and your education adviser from the White House are going to be on all the talk radio and television shows in town, being interviewed in the newspapers."

In the Reagan White House, Deaver explains, keeping the message as clear and effective as possible took months of planning:

> We always had a strategic plan. It began with the 100-day plan that we started through the transition under Ed Meese's supervision and ran through the first 100 days. We had a slight blip when the President got shot, but that plan basically stuck as a governing communications plan.

> After that, we organized something which we called the Blair House group, which met every Friday and took the schedule out for three months and picked what the message of the day was going to be for every day for the next three months. When we got to the last two weeks, we worked on every hour so that by the time a day in the President's life came, we were pretty well-organized on what that message was going to be.

> Our goal was that we wanted to go to bed at night knowing what above-the-fold in *The New York Times*

and *The Washington Post* was going to be, not having to wake up the next morning and make what was above the fold in *The Washington Post* and *The New York Times* run our day. We did everything we could to have that strategic plan to keep the message simple, the repetition and the discipline.

The Clinton White House, says Towson University Professor of Political Science Martha Kumar, has been successful in developing a campaign-style version of this tight form of coordination:

> On the issue of crime, they brought together a variety of people. Dick Morris was the one who would identify that as an important issue. Mark Penn did the polling. Bruce Reed, who was in the domestic policy shop, would find the policy mode that they would work with. Don Baer would write the speech, and Rahm Emmanuel would set up the event and decide what kinds of players to bring together to be with the President and back up a particular issue. So they have had a flexibility that I think other administrations will use.

> Is all of this bad? We seem to often have a view that communications is not substance, that communications is some form of legerdemain. It is not. Communication is central to governing. If you can't communicate, you can't lead, and it is something that an administration should pay attention to and that we should encourage them to do.

Barry Toiv, who was Bill Clinton's deputy press secretary, notes that the early failure of the Clinton team to emulate Deaver's style of tight coordination and discipline undermined the President's efforts to build support for his most important issues:

> Part of the problem was that the President got sidetracked by a couple of issues that were not central to his campaign and were not going to be central to his presidency.

> But the bigger problem was the lack of discipline over the schedule and the message. The President often had ... several public events in one day, and he also was talking to the press a lot in an unplanned way and a very casual, offhanded way. After an event, he'd be working the rope line, and if he was asked a question, he'd answer it, if he was asked a question by the press that was there by the rope line. In doing that, he would often detract from whatever message it was he was trying to convey that day. It just didn't work. There was too much going on.

Only when Clinton appointed Leon Panetta as Chief of Staff was the Clinton communications strategy put back on track, says Toiv. Panetta and his deputies pared back Clinton's schedule and introduced more discipline into the White House operation.

Coordinating a Communications Strategy

But while discipline and coordination are important, Toiv argues, it makes sense to separate communications from message development:

> When you're talking communications, you're talking mainly the kinds of things that Mike [McCurry] was talking about. You're talking about developing a message, scheduling around that message, trying to mobilize the American people in support of those themes and that message and that agenda. The press function is dealing with the press corps. It's the day-to-day, week-to-week, month-to-month dealing with the questions of the press, trying to sell—"sell" may not be the right word, but trying to advocate what the President is doing with the press, trying to work with them on their stories, just all the things that press secretaries do.

> Those are really two different functions. In the beginning of the Clinton Administration, they were all combined into one shop and it did not work, because you just could not expect the leadership of that office to do all those things and do them successfully. They realized that eventually. Of course, in the White House everybody's a communications director and everybody's a press secretary. Everybody's talking to the press whether they admit it or not. ... But if there's discipline, that's fine, because then it's not a big problem. Anyway, all these functions were put into one office.

Toiv also stresses the importance of keeping the press secretary firmly in the White House loop:

> Do empower your press secretary. Dee Dee Myers was really not well served by the structure in the White House, because she could not do as easily what Mike [McCurry] following her, and then Joe [Lockhart] following him, could do: Walk in anywhere, any time, and get whatever information they need, whether it was from the chief of staff or walking into the Oval Office and talking to the President. In the half hour before a briefing, the press secretary needs to walk into the Oval Office. I think that the press secretary really needs to be empowered to do that, and to sit in on policy meetings, both foreign and domestic policy, to get a better understanding

of the policy and to know what's coming up around the bend.

Toiv offers a series of dos and don'ts that he says the next White House team would do well to remember, in order to create a good public impression of the President:

- Do enforce discipline.

- Don't undermine each other and your President with the dreaded negative or political background quote, or the unauthorized leak that will just kill a good initiative.

- Do work as a team in terms of message and in talking to reporters, not only on the record, but also for off-the-record and background conversations.

- Let each other know who's working on what story. These are all pretty basic, but sometimes they just don't happen.

- Don't forget who's President. When you're talking to the press, remember: The President makes policy; you don't.

- Don't tolerate excessive leaks, but don't establish a thought police.

- Do make your President accessible.

- Do not just be reactive. Be aggressive. There's a tendency, with all the questions pouring in, to just be reactive. You've got to be aggressive, and that requires planning.

- Do start fresh. Don't be afraid to do something new, but watch out for the White House press corps, because if you make changes that they perceive as being aimed at them or something that affects their lifestyle, they're going to be paying a lot of attention to it.

- Be nice. McCurry and Lockhart have both made a major point of this. The press is no different from anybody else. They want their needs met. They want to get on the air. They want to get into print. So you need to give them something to report on. They need critical facts on deadline. Get them. They want fair warning of schedules and travel. Give it to them. The space they have is remarkably small to work in, so be sympathetic. Be patient. They want to be able to tell their parents they got to spend time with the President. Make sure they spend time with the President. When you visit their hometown, make sure their family gets to meet the President. Little things matter a lot to reporters, as they would to everybody.

- Don't be arrogant.

Landon Parvin

THE ROLE OF SPEECHES

It is important to recognize the vital importance of presidential speeches in the process of creating a strong impression in the public's mind about a President and his agenda. Landon Parvin, who wrote speeches for Ronald Reagan, says that the presidential speech, if designed to capture the imagination, is a powerful tool to shape opinion:

> Have something big to sell. Advocate big things that will define a presidency, not incremental things that will diminish it.
>
> Since I do a lot of corporate work, I am constantly reading the business press, and I have noticed something interesting. When they ask CEOs who have successfully turned around major corporations what they would have done differently, almost without fail they say that they wish they had taken larger, more dramatic actions sooner.
>
> I would argue that the same lesson holds for a President and his programs. Overlooking the fact that President Clinton's original health care plan would have been a disaster, the President did exactly the right thing in proposing something big, and I am sure the Clinton speechwriters felt good selling something so substantial.

Carol Gelderman, Professor of English at the University of New Orleans, has studied the way in which Presidents use speeches to communicate their ideas to the public. She adds that in addition to capturing the imagination, successful Presidents also use speeches to educate the public:

> That was certainly the essence of what Franklin Roosevelt thought he was doing, which was teaching. He said the greatest duty of a statesman was to teach, and he called his budget his textbook. He called the place where he had his press conferences his schoolroom. He called his fireside chats his "seminars." I was quite surprised when I learned that he had only given 27 of these fireside chats.

The President should view the speechwriting team not just as hired wordsmiths, adds Parvin, but also as a valuable sounding board in the development of the initiatives the President intends to propose:

> I would urge a President to fill his White House not only with the tactful, pleasant people you need for jobs like congressional or public liaison, but with crusaders, ideologues, pragmatists, contrarians, reformers, and interesting intellectuals, because without these people, who in the White House will debate and advocate and fight and cause change?

> In the Reagan White House, the speechwriters saw themselves as the keepers of the Reagan flame. Although I was no longer on staff, this was especially true in Reagan's second term.

Michael Waldman, Bill Clinton's former chief speechwriter, agrees on the importance of this:

> The strongest thing that I can argue to any administration, is the vital importance of linking speeches and speechwriting on the one hand and policy on the other, with the President in the middle of it. The gravest mistake that any White House can make is to view speeches as merely the way you sell a program, as distinct from and divorced from the formation of the program: speechwriting as, in effect, the advertising copywriters off in a different room, and we will let them know what they are supposed to write about, and they will pretty up the words.

By understanding this, adds Waldman, a President can use the combination of policy and key words to change the politics of an issue. He cites Social Security as an example:

> The best example that I can think of to show the power of that is in the 1998 State of the Union, which, as you may recall, was a time of great drama for reasons having nothing to do with the budget of that year. There were brand new numbers indicating a budget surplus for the first time, and the President got up and said, "What should we do with our new surplus? I have a simple, straightforward answer: Save Social Security first."

> The Democrats jumped up and applauded during the State of the Union, and they were applauding just about anything by that point. Speaker [Newt] Gingrich mulled it over for a moment, and then he stood up and applauded. The Republicans in Congress looked at each other and stood up and applauded, and at that moment a trillion dollars

shifted in the budget silently from tax cuts to Social Security.

Gelderman adds that many Presidents have understood well the importance of the close relationship between a policymaker and his speechwriter, and speeches tend to go badly when this kind of close cooperation does not exist:

> Eisenhower believed there also had to be a chief of staff of the speech, whatever the speech was about. He felt there had to be one person who is the conduit for everything .... When he wrote the Atoms for Peace speech, the drafting of that speech lasted seven and a half months and went through 33 drafts, and all kinds of people were consulted in the Atomic Energy Commission, in the State Department, in the Pentagon, and in the White House .... This whole process never would have worked had he not appointed one person to be in charge of this whole thing.

> [Y]ou could make the same case for Lyndon Johnson when he made that speech on March 31, 1968 ... that was his speech that completely turned around his Vietnam policy. It was a 180-degree turn. That speech started because he had a need to respond to this Tet offensive. He said the end was in sight just before this horrible Tet offensive. That speech took two and a half months, went through many drafts, and, again, he had a person appointed, Harry McPherson, who was the conduit through whom everybody passed everything.

> Kennedy did the same thing in the Cuban missile crisis. He had 14 people he appointed, his inner circle—he called them "ex-com"—just for the 13 days that they worked on this. He put Ted Sorensen in charge of all that, and Sorensen said at the end that it was the writing of the speech and the fact that somebody is taking notes, somebody is paying attention at the end of every meeting, so that you can see that there is some kind of progress.

THE PROBLEM OF MEDIA COVERAGE

Michael Deaver designed Ronald Reagan's highly effective communications strategy. But, as he points out, significant differences exist between the media industry Reagan dealt with and the industry a President faces today:

> We had, as we used to say, three "nets" and CNN at that time. It was really four networks, but we were still trying to get used to CNN being considered a network.

How that's changed. We had two news cycles we worked from, the noon news cycle and the evening news cycle. Today, everybody is on the Net. Instead of a bevy of Lily Tomlins plugging in calls at the White House, they have a bevy of people who are on computers, directly getting into reporters who are writing stories to give their second graph of each story. There are not two news cycles today, but a 24-hour news cycle. And there are not three nets or four nets; there are 50 news channels running, some of them 24 hours a day.

Toiv points out the difference this made for Bill Clinton:

When the Reagan White House wanted to communicate to the American people about the important vote coming up in the Congress on his economic program or a tax program, a tax bill, they were able to call the networks and say, "We want to do an Oval Office address in prime time." I'm sure it wasn't as easy then as it seems to us to have been now, but President Reagan was able to do that at key moments in the legislative debate and have a major impact.

No more. It won't happen. I don't have a list of the times that President Clinton was able to do it, but believe me, if there's just a vote coming up in the Congress on a question that's important to him, he's not going to be able to get on the air on the broadcast networks. The cable networks, sometimes yes, sometimes no. Except in a real crisis, they just won't do it.

But while getting national media attention may be difficult for a President, former Speaker of the House Newt Gingrich's press secretary, Tony Blankley, reminds us that the President still has a built-in advantage over his possible critics on Capitol Hill:

While it's true that every Congressman and every Senator has a press secretary, and some have a few, almost all of them don't work on national issues. They're working their hometown press, bragging about bringing home a bridge bill or whatever it is. They don't focus on the national issues. They don't focus on the national press. And you have a very big mismatch to the White House's advantage between about a third of the White House, which either through press, communications, advance, press advance, is focused on communicating the message to the media, through the media to the public, and on the congressional side, about a half a dozen press secretaries to leadership officials in the House and the Senate of each party who spend most of their time focusing on dealing with the national press.

I think you're going to see a slow balancing, or a closing of the imbalance, over the coming years as Congress builds up a bigger staff to deal with the press, particularly because you have the existence of the White House team, which simply inundates you with manpower, and because of the tapeworm, as you say, the need to feed the ever-expanding media.

The difficulty today of commanding press attention for an important policy proposal does limit the President's ability to build support for his agenda. But, says Deaver, the President can still get national press attention on his terms when he is proposing a major initiative:

If the President of the United States has news, it's going to be covered. Now, whether it's going to blanket the three nets, which now have, what, 28 percent of the audience—no wonder they're worried about giving the President of the United States some time—part of it has to do with ... building the interest from a news standpoint—and, secondly, having an issue that's a concern, real concern, to all Americans.

I think, frankly, with the Clinton Administration, after the health care debates, there never was a big domestic issue. If you're going to talk about school uniforms and commuter traffic every day instead of proposing major changes like Social Security or changing the IRS—I still think those are two issues that, if you worked it right and built it and were committed to that instead of a long list during an hour-and-a-half State of the Union every year, you could generate a television interest in covering a speech.

Veteran journalist Robert Novak, however, argues that a President can no longer plan on major media coverage for even major announcements:

I guarantee you, if the President of the United States said, "We're coming up to a vote on Social Security, and we're going to have an Oval Office speech on Social Security because the bill is coming up," he would have a strikeout. It would have to be a Monica Lewinsky story or a bombing of Iraq story or something of that nature.

One of the reasons is you have this small percentage of the share by the broadcast networks compared to the old days, and they know that this is going to be broadcast on Fox; it's going to be broadcast on

MSNBC; it's going to be broadcast on CNN. They know it's going to be done. So you're taking a small share of people who would really pass up basketball and the smarmy prime-time programs on the broadcast network to watch the Social Security speech. That's going to be further divided up among the cable networks.

On the other hand, says Martha Kumar, the State of the Union Address offers a unique opportunity for a major policy statement to command media attention. She notes that the Clinton Administration has shown how to exploit that opportunity fully by presenting the speech as part of a carefully orchestrated communications strategy:

Carl Cannon, Tony Blankley, and Martha Kumar

> What the Clinton Administration has done is, the State of the Union they treat as a different kind of speech in that it's a two-month event. When the Congress leaves town, they take the media for two months, for the month of December and January, and the Congress, with all its press secretaries, has not been able to really get into those stories in the way that they have done it.
>
> They start out with, say, an interview with *The New York Times* or with the President holding a large press conference, as he did in the State Department, where he talked about his issues for the coming year and governing and his leadership. And then it moved week by week, one issue after another. Education one week, Social Security another.
>
> They were able to take that speech and turn it into a two-month event that truly set out their agenda. So perhaps they don't need that Oval Office address in quite the same way, because they're hitting it over that time period, and the public gets a sense of what they are doing.

TECHNIQUES TO GAIN FAVORABLE COVERAGE

Recent Presidents who have been successful in using the press, like Clinton, have recognized that although the media is more chaotic and less in awe of the presidency than ever before, a President still has techniques and innovations available to him that he can use to build public support through the press. The experts point to several approaches.

Using the "Gaggle." The morning gaggle occurs when the press secretary brings the White House press corps into his office, usually around 9:30 a.m., for an informal 20-minute question-and-answer session. This early meeting with journalists, says Barry Toiv, can be helpful to the President's staff:

> The gaggle helps you to prepare for the briefing, because you know what's on the minds of the press, and if the press is having an event, the President is going to be exposed to the press that day, it allows you to alert the President to what questions he might get.

Novak agrees that the gaggle is a useful device for the President:

> I really believe that the gaggle is a great advantage for the Clinton White House. I think it's going to be used by either the Bush White House or the Gore White House, because they put out the message every morning, and reporters all over town who don't go to the gaggle are watching the news, the cable networks, to find out what it is.

The Clinton White House, says Kumar, has skillfully combined the creation of its own news with the use of the gaggle and the regular press briefing:

> Considering the changes [inherent in] a 24-hour news day … the briefing has a somewhat different nature than what it had earlier. The way the Clinton communications operation works, they give out news over a period of time. They really try to go back to the model that you all had and get a story running and have it running for several days, so that a story will be dropped as an exclusive early on. For example, if there's a computer story, a technology story, a medical health story, that often will appear as an exclusive in *USA Today*.
>
> Then there's a discussion of it in the gaggle in the morning, and then, by the time the briefing comes, what happens in the briefing is rather than announcing policy, as so often happened in the past, it's a discussion of the politics of the particular policy. And that has a very different kind of tone to it, because it ends up being a contentious kind of event

rather than one where maybe the straight substance is given. But it has been a trade-off that's worked for them, because they've been able to get a longer attention span on a story than would normally be the case.

Because the briefing is televised, the gaggle gives an opportunity not only to give a story earlier, but also to work out some of the kinds of issues that might exist between the White House and the press in an informal kind of environment. Those are exchanges that need to take place, such as when the press secretary announces the schedule.

"Bouncing Off" the News. Bill Clinton is a master at turning the news cycle to his advantage and using it to reinforce his key legislative goals. For example, he shaped his responses to school shootings to emphasize gun control, and he linked various HMO news stories to his demand for "patient bill of rights" legislation. As Barry Toiv notes:

The networks do not cover the President as much as they used to, but they still follow a good story. The networks … are doing a huge number of stories on health care. That's what people care about. The White House does a lot of events on health care, and the connection works sometimes.

They still love to follow conflict, to follow a good story. The war of words that's been going on between the President and the NRA [National Rifle Association], that's a pretty good story, and they're covering it like crazy. The President did—I think he's done three events in the last week or so on gun control, and they'll just keep right on doing it, and hopefully we'll have accomplished something from the White House point of view, actually move legislation or make Republicans pay pretty badly for not moving legislation. That's something that the press will continue to cover.

Adopting Novel Approaches to Cultivate the Media. During his first campaign for President, Bill Clinton recognized that he needed to find new ways to reach key audiences. Playing the saxophone and appearing on MTV were among his more startling gambits. But, as Kumar points out, Clinton also has demonstrated that there are more mundane but highly effective ways of cultivating important journalists:

Clinton, in a session that he had with weather forecasters in 1997, talked about what his role as President was today and how difficult it is to create a consensus. He said that it's important in the case of global warming, that we need to get a sense among the people, and he used the weather forecasters, brought them in to have them have a sense of it so they could talk on their news programs or talk on their weather programs, "Because our country always gets it right. We always get it right once we focus on it. But right now, while the scientists see the train coming down the tunnel, most Americans don't hear the whistle blowing. They don't sense that it's out there, that it's an issue. I really believe as President, one of my most important jobs is to tell the American people what the big issues are that we have to deal with. If we understand what the issues are, if we start with a certain set of principles, we always come out to the right place."

Using Press Conferences. Another way a President can gain an upper hand, says Robert Novak, is to make greater use of press conferences:

One of the do's, I think, is regular press conferences. I can't understand why people as smart as Nixon, as Clinton, even Reagan, had such infrequent press conferences. One of the arguments is, "It takes so much to prepare for them." Well, it does when you have one every six months, but if you have a regular press conference, it's not that big a deal, and the President almost always comes out on top. So I would say regular press conferences would be a very helpful thing.

Still, not everyone thinks that it is wise for the President to play the 24-hour-a-day news cycle game. For example, veteran journalist Sander Vanocur says:

I happen to be a believer in the presidency being a slightly distant place, to invoke awe and respect and a little bit of mysticism, so the advice I have to the next President of the United States is, he should set the rules. Call in the heads of the networks, the news services, major newspapers, magazines, and say, "This is what I'm going to do." It could be a weekly news conference. It could be a monthly news conference. It could be a conference every two months. But set the rules and stick with them.

I know the Clinton Administration has been very good at dealing with the media, rapid-fire response and everything, but I would urge the next President of the United States to go back to square one. Set the rules. Say "I'm not going to be a recluse, but I'm not going to be on call 24 hours a day to answer your demands, because they'll never end." I think, in so doing, he'll have the respect and admiration of the American people, who don't much admire the media.

COMMUNICATING THE MESSAGE TO KEY GROUPS

In addition to appealing to the public as a whole, to be successful the President must also appeal to key groups and constituencies, and garner their support. Presidents rely on groups that generally support them to build public and press support for their programs. The staffs of the White House Office of Public Liaison and the Office of Political Liaison energize grassroots supporters and build support among other constituencies.

Lyn Nofziger and Ed Meese

Lyn Nofziger headed the Office of Political Liaison for Ronald Reagan. He says, however, that Richard Nixon had a better model for the office, since Reagan's unique personal popularity meant the office had an unusual advantage. Under Nixon, the Office's machinery had to be more systematic:

> President Nixon understood that he was not a popular person, that he was not a lovable person, and that he would have to work to get the American people to accept him and to accept the things he wanted to do. So he brought in Chuck Colson. I suppose that would be the first public liaison office, or one of the early ones. Chuck's job was to deal with all the organizations out in the country, the various special groups such as the Chambers of Commerce, the National Association of Manufacturers (NAM), the cotton growers, the automobile manufacturers, and so forth, and work with them to get them to understand what it was the President was trying to do and to support him in doing those things.
>
> Chuck, before he got religion, was pretty rough about these things. He utilized the Cabinet officers to make sure that those organizations out in the country knew what they could expect from this administration if they cooperated—and knew what

they could expect from this administration if they did not cooperate.

Under Reagan, the Office of Political Liaison's duty was more to fan support among the faithful, according to Nofziger:

> In the Reagan White House, we concentrated primarily—my shop did—on making sure that the political people out in the country were aware of what the President wanted and moved to support him through various ways, through issuing their own press releases, making their own speeches, so that you had an ongoing drumbeat from the political people, or from the Republican Party, out to the country so that it was just not the President speaking alone.

Anne Wexler, who headed the Office of Public Liaison for Jimmy Carter, echoes Nofziger in emphasizing that the liaison offices must not be seen as a White House equivalent of congressional caseworkers. Instead, she says, they should be part of an integrated team that develops and advocates the President's policies:

> From my point of view, and from the point of view of the Carter White House, the Office of Public Liaison is put together to essentially support the priority issues of the President, to build public support for those issues, and that ... makes it a coordination job. The Office of Public Liaison is the place where all the people who work in the White House have to come together as a team, essentially, to try to work together to formulate and then sell the priority issues of the President.

> What the Office of Public Liaison is not is a casework office for constituencies. Sometimes it's perceived as being that, but it is not and should not be. It essentially has two parallel functions. One is advocacy, and I'll talk a little bit about that. The other is, as has been mentioned previously, education.

> So on the one hand, the Office of Public Liaison is working very closely with other offices in the White House to build an advocacy program for the President's issues. At the same time, on the other parallel track, it's doing the educating. It's bringing in people for briefings; it's responding to people who ask for briefings; and it's reaching out to constituencies to educate them on those issues.

Routine constituent work is of course important, says Wexler, but keeping it separate from the work of the Public Liaison can be beneficial for everyone:

One of the other things that I think helped the Carter White House in terms of its outreach and advocacy was the fact that there were people who did constituent work in the White House, but they did not report to the Assistant to the President for Public Liaison. We had a group of deputy assistants to the President who did seniors, Hispanics, consumers, ethnics, African-Americans, Jewish Americans. They all had a direct reporting relationship to the President. I don't think that they met with the President that often, but the groups that they reported to and worked with knew that they had a direct reporting relationship, and it made it a lot easier for the Office of Public Liaison to do the job that it was supposed to do.

Most experts agree that the Office of Public Liaison should be fully integrated into the White House operation as part of a unified strategy. In so doing, it should work in tandem with the congressional relations and communications staff. Wexler puts it this way:

Linking policy and the speechwriters is probably one of the most important things that you can do. The speechwriters had to be an integral part, with the policy people, in the teams that we put together to work on these issues. The Office of Intergovernmental Relations, the Cabinet Secretary and the Cabinet, and OMB all were advocates for presidential programs and priorities, and all of them played a role in a coordinated scenario.

We did run these coordinated scenarios for priority issues as task forces. There was one person who was in charge, there was a lot of tracking and accountability, and people learned how to work together. It was a learning curve in the Carter Administration.

Wexler also points out that in the same way that it is important to bring speechwriters into the policy development discussion, because they have a feel for how a proposal will be received, it is important to have a two-way discussion with key groups to gauge their reception to proposals. Wexler convened a regular weekly lunch during the Carter Administration for this purpose:

People from OMB and the Council of Economic Advisers and the policy groups through our office were constantly meeting with groups to try to find out what they were thinking and how they would respond to the things that the policy groups were working on.

I did one thing that I don't think has been done in a regular way since, which I found very useful and I think others, particularly the President, found useful. I had a group of people from the outside who came to the White House every Wednesday for lunch. They had lunch in the Roosevelt Room every Wednesday. They were essentially people who had been White House aides in the Johnson Administration. There were some lobbyists, a couple of people who were heads of trade associations. It was an eclectic group.

We met every Wednesday for three years. There was never a story in the paper about this group. None of the people who came ever talked about what we talked about inside. But they were our window in a very real way to the outside world, and there was a lot of very frank conversation that went on about what was going on in the White House, what people were saying on the street, how they could help.

The meetings were attended, interestingly enough, usually by one person from the policy shop, occasionally by someone from congressional liaison, but always by the speechwriters, who were very interested in hearing the feedback of what was going on. After each lunch, I would write a memo to the President saying, "Here is what they said this week." And after a while, the President would call on Wednesdays and say, "Well, what did they say today?" Sometimes they were helpful and sometimes they were critical, but the information that came in, because it was very frank, was very helpful.

Sichan Siv, who served in the Office of Public Liaison under President Bush, points out that such feedback, when given to the policy or speechwriting staff, can lead to subtle changes that make all the difference to key groups:

I recall a meeting I had with the Japanese-Americans on the 50th anniversary of Pearl Harbor. I brought in a lot of people, including the members of the 442nd Regiment, who fought in World War II. I also included one speechwriter. We were talking about Japanese-Americans, and one gentleman rose and said, "We are not Japanese-Americans. We are Americans of Japanese ancestry."

I looked at the speechwriter, he put it down, and when Bush went to Pearl Harbor to speak at the 50th anniversary, he said "Americans of Japanese ancestry." That was a very strong point, because they all considered they are Americans first and everything else second.

According to those who have served in the Office of Public Liaison, the office can also accept responsibility when the President is unable to deliver something to a constituency group. If the office is doing its job well, in other words, it can defuse potential problems with key groups.

Speakers List

White House & Government

Martin Anderson
>Former Assistant to the President for Policy Development, President Reagan

Gary Andres
>Former Deputy Assistant to the President for Legislative Affairs, President Bush

Veronica Biggins
>Former Director of the Office of Presidential Personnel, President Clinton

Tony Blankley
>Former Press Secretary to Speaker of the House Gingrich

Zbigniew Brzezinski
>Former National Security Adviser to President Carter

James Burnley
>Former Secretary of Transportation to President Reagan

Gerald Carmen
>Former Administrator of the General Services Administration, President Reagan

Michael Deaver
>Former Assistant to the President and Deputy Chief of Staff, President Reagan

Donald Devine
>Former Director of the Office of Personnel Management, President Reagan

C. Boyden Gray
>Former Counsel, President Bush

Pat Griffin
>Former Assistant to and Director of Legislative Affairs, President Clinton

E. Pendleton James
>Former Director of the Office of Presidential Personnel, President Reagan

Kelly D. Johnston
Former Secretary of the United States Senate, 104th Congress

Steven Kelman
Administrator of the Office of Federal Procurement (OMB),
President Clinton

James King
Former Director of the Office of Personnel Management,
President Clinton

Charles Kolb
Former Deputy Assistant for Domestic Policy, President Bush

Tom Korologos
Former Deputy Assistant for Senate Relations, Presidents
Nixon and Ford

Edwin Meese III
Former Counsellor, President Reagan

George Nesterczuk
Former Staff Director of the House Subcommittee on Civil
Service

Lyn Nofziger
Former Assistant to the President for Political Affairs,
President Reagan

Leon Panetta
Former Chief of Staff, President Clinton

Landon Parvin
Speechwriter, President Reagan

Peter Rodman
Former Deputy Assistant to the President for National
Security Affairs, President Reagan

Sichan Siv
Deputy Assistant to the President for Public Liaison,
President Bush

Theodore C. Sorensen
Former Counsel, President Kennedy

Barry Toiv
Former Deputy Press Secretary to President Clinton

Chase Untermeyer
Former Director of the Office of Presidential Personnel,
President Bush

Jack Valenti
Former Special Assistant, President Johnson

Michael Waldman
    Speechwriter, President Clinton

Jack Watson
    Former Chief of Staff, President Carter

Caspar Weinberger
    Former Secretary of Defense, President Reagan

Anne Wexler
    Former Assistant to the President for Public Liaison,
    President Carter

Joseph Wright
    Former Director of the Office of Management and Budget for
    President Reagan

Media

Michael Barone
    Senior Writer, *U.S. News & World Report*

Helle Bering
    Editor of the Editorial Page, *The Washington Times*

Carl Cannon
    Government Executive Editor, *National Journal*

Richard Cohen
    Congressional Reporter, *National Journal*

Helen Dewar
    Senate Reporter, *The Washington Post*

Albert Eisele
    Editor, *The Hill*

Bob Franken
    Congressional Correspondent, CNN

John Harris
    White House Correspondent, *The Washington Post*

Charles Krauthammer
    Syndicated Columnist

Donald Lambro
    Chief Political Correspondent, *The Washington Times*

Robert Novak
    Syndicated Columnist

Alexis Simendinger
    White House Correspondent, *National Journal*

Ken Smith
    Deputy Editor of the Editorial Page, *The Washington Times*

Karen Tumulty
White House Correspondent, *Time Magazine*

Sander Vanocur
Former NBC Television Correspondent

Fareed Zakaria
Managing Editor, *Foreign Affairs*

Academia & Public Policy

John Burke
Professor of Politics, University of Vermont

Colin Campbell
Professor of Public Policy, Georgetown University

Carol Gelderman
Professor, University of New Orleans

Ed Gillespie
Former Director of Communications and Congressional
Affairs, Republican National Committee

Stephen Hess
Senior Fellow in Government Studies, The Brookings
Institution

Robert Kagan
Carnegie Endowment for International Peace

Martha Kumar
Professor of Political Science, Towson University

Paul Light
Vice President, Director of Government Studies, The
Brookings Institution

Robert Maranto
Professor, Villanova University

Richard E. Neustadt
Professor Emeritus, Harvard University

James P. Pfiffner
Professor of Government and Public Policy, George Mason
University

Georgia Sorenson
James MacGregor Burns Academy of Leadership, University
of Maryland

James A. Thurber
Center for Congressional and Presidential Studies, American
University

Susan J. Tolchin
    Professor of Public Policy, George Mason University

Shirley Anne Warshaw
    Professor of Political Science, Gettysburg College